SHINE
like
STARS

Becoming a Light to the World
A STUDY OF PHILIPPIANS

SHINE
like
STARS

Becoming a Light to the World
A STUDY OF PHILIPPIANS

BY SARA B. LEIGHTON

Gospel Advocate Company
Nashville, Tennessee

Published by Gospel Advocate Co.
1006 Elm Hill Pike, Nashville, TN 37210
http://www.gospeladvocate.com

ISBN: 0-89225-542-0

DEDICATION

Dedicated to the men in my life who have fueled, trimmed and magnified my light: Loyd L. Brian, my dad; James, my husband; and Brian and Bob, my sons.

Special thanks to the ladies of the Ethridge Church of Christ who shared observations and life experiences during our study of Philippians and to William E. Woodson and David Stofel for critiquing my manuscript.

TABLE OF CONTENTS

Introduction 9

1 Light for a Desert Pathway 11

2 The Forget-Me-Nots of the Angels 17

3 Ye Quenchless Stars! 23

4 Stars Hide Your Fires 29

5 Harmony of the Stars 37

6 Sun of My Soul 45

7 Like Stars in the Universe 53

8 Hovering 'Twixt Night and Morn 63

9 Fixed to a Star 71

10 Wandering Stars 79

11 Peace Divine Like Quiet Night 87

12 Shimmering Stars, Shining Souls 95

13 Setting Our Course by a High Star 103

Works Cited 111

WHY PHILIPPIANS?

My favorite New Testament book is Philippians. More meat is compacted in this little book and its potent verses than in any other. Paul was a master letter writer – we can learn much from him about the lost art of writing thank you notes! Beyond that, however, we can learn so much more about living for Christ.

In Philippians, Paul was a man of few words, but, oh, what words! Because he was elderly at the time he wrote Philippians and suffering the persecution of imprisonment, he understood the importance of the joy, peace and comfort that Christ brings to His faithful followers. This is especially true when those blessings are compounded by the joy, peace and comfort of supportive Christian brothers and sisters. Paul loved the Philippian church, the only church recorded in the New Testament from which Paul accepted monetary help.

Many short, succinct gems of truth in Philippians should be a part of the memorized repertoire of every Christian (see suggested memory work in the "Above and Beyond" sections). Keeping such jewels always ready on the lips will help sustain anyone facing difficulty.

However, it is the heart of his message to the Philippians that makes me choose this letter as my personal favorite above all others. I need this book. By nature I am not a gentle and humble person. Like many Christian women in today's world, I have been given authority in the secular world that can easily swallow up the gentle, quiet nature God demands of us. Although I am not in a corporate position as many women are today, I am a teacher of 16- to 18-year-old high school students – a position that demands respect for authority if the job is to be done well. My age, my demeanor and my voice – although I hope not strident – tell my students that I am in charge in my classroom. How easy it is to take my schoolteacher voice home with me!

The decisions I must make affecting my students' futures demand a strong-willed person, a woman who is not easily intimidated – a "steel magnolia" in today's vernacular. The Philippian church also had its strong-willed women: Lydia, who must have held a position of authority as a retailer of fine fabrics, and Syntyche and Euodia, the faithful, dedicated workers in the Philippian church who couldn't get along with each other. Sound familiar? It certainly does to me. It is so easy to become contentious, power-hungry and self-important when the lives we live, the decisions we make, and the work we do feeds that ill-nature in us.

Philippians is a letter that a Christian woman can truly take to heart. Paul teaches that all I do on the job, at home and in the community must be tempered with love, joy, peace, gentleness and humility. I must show that God works in me to will and to act according to His purpose (Philippians 2:13). I must show that Christ lives in me every day and in every way. Keeping Paul's words to the Philippians continuously before me is a way of tempering my will to His will. Only then will I shine like a star holding out the Word of Life.

A CLEARER FOCUS

1. List positions of authority you hold outside your home and the church.

2. List negative traits arising from your activities or positions of authority.

3. Is it more difficult for a woman to keep her secular work from bleeding over into her home and church life than it is for a man? Why or why not?

1

LIGHT FOR A DESERT PATHWAY

"Follow you the star that lights a desert pathway, yours or mine.
Forward, till you see the Highest Human Nature is divine."
– Alfred, Lord Tennyson

Whenever my husband and I take a vacation or business trip, I like to learn as much as possible about the area we are visiting before I go. A little background research increases my appreciation and understanding. Historical and geographical context is just as important when we study the Bible. Let's tour the ancient city of Philippi and meet its citizens.

Geographically, Philippi was a mountain-pass town in the range of peaks separating Europe and Asia. Its ruins still can be seen today in Greece near the town of Kavala (formerly, Neapolis) on the Aegean Sea. Philippi was an important stopover on the main road, the Via Egnatia, connecting Rome to its provinces in Asia and the Palestinian region. It was located on the Gangitis River 10 miles north of the seaport town of Neapolis where ships continually launched and landed, carrying travelers to and from Troas in Asia. Philippi was surrounded by fertile soil, and several silver and gold mines brought in huge revenues to the area.

Philippi was first fortified in 358 B.C. by the father of Alexander the Great, King Philip II of Macedonia, for whom the city was named. In 42 B.C., it became the site of a famous battle in which Octavian and Antony defeated Brutus and Cassius who had murdered Julius Caesar. Octavian was later known as Caesar Augustus, the first emperor of Rome, whose taxation is mentioned in Luke 2:1 at the birth of Christ. After the victory, Octavian made Philippi into a miniature Rome, complete with acropolis, forum, palestra, agora and amphitheater. And yes, he built a Roman prison complete with dungeons and stocks.

Think of Philippi as the retirement home of Roman military personnel. Many old soldiers were granted land in the area and settled there, giving the city the ambiance of military import found in ancient Rome. The citizens dressed, acted and looked Roman; and Latin, of course, was the official language. Meanwhile, the local folks of Hellenistic ancestry still spoke Greek as the common man's language. Within this European mix lived a small contingency of Jews whose religion was officially registered with and permitted by the Roman government. Their numbers were so small that no synagogue had been built; therefore, they met on the Sabbath for prayer beside the Gangitis River.

Events of Acts 16

Christianity was unheard of in Europe and, therefore, was not a recognized or sanctioned religion. Enter Paul on his second missionary trip with his entourage, which included Silas and Timothy as well as Luke, evidenced by his use of first person narrative in Acts 16 beginning at Troas. Paul had wanted to teach and preach in Asia but was prohibited from doing so by God (Acts 16:6). Instead, a man from Macedonia came to Paul in a vision and begged him to come there to teach the Europeans. Sailing from Troas to Neapolis, Paul and his companions arrived by foot at Philippi.

Finding no synagogue in which to teach Jews the gospel, the travelers joined a group gathered for Sabbath prayer by the river. There Paul fell into conversation with Lydia, a businesswoman originally from

Thyatira in the region of Lydia (perhaps the origin of her name) who was now living and working in Philippi. Lydia was a retailer of fine fabrics. What she sold was not cheap; probably it was the best cloth money could buy. Purple was considered a royal color, the dyes produced by crushing thousands of tiny sea snails, a laborious and painstaking task. Labor, although cheap, would have inflated the price. Her linens were also fine – not the coarse, scratchy fabric that the less affluent serving class wore. Indeed, Lydia was a prosperous woman in a prosperous business. This is further attested to by the house that she maintained in Philippi – a house large enough to accommodate the growing number of converts to Christianity for worship, including those in her own household.

It is often said that money talks. Such was the case of a slave girl possessed by a demon. She made money for her owners by telling fortunes (Acts 16:16). She followed Paul and his companions around for several days, repeatedly shouting that they were representatives of God with a message of salvation. Finally, troubled by the poor girl's plight, Paul rebuked the demon; it left her, and she became quiet. The story should have had a happy ending, but again, money talks. Her owners were so enraged at losing their livelihood that they grabbed Paul and Silas, dragged them before the city magistrates, and falsely accused them of causing a commotion by teaching customs that were unlawful under Roman law. As usual, idlers were standing by who were easily incited to join a cause, whether through mob dynamics or bribery. In the heat of the moment, the authorities demanded that the two miscreants be stripped and flogged. They were probably tied to a whipping post in the marketplace and beaten with a bundle of rods or canes, similar to a practice called "caning" in Asian countries today.

Paul and Silas were then thrown into prison with a stern command to the jailer to guard them carefully. Not one to be thought of as soft and unable to carry out his duties, the jailer put them in the maximum security cell – the lowest, darkest portion of the prison. He had them placed in stocks, sitting in a tortuous slumped-forward position with ankles and wrists securely fastened for ultimate discomfort. Imagine the pain – a raw, mutilated, bleeding, exposed back and no way to ease the pain, tend the wounds, or relieve the ache! In such a position, I probably would have cried and felt sorry for myself, but not Paul and Silas. They prayed and, of all things, sang!

A violent earthquake, so prevalent even today in that area, shook the prison, unfastened the doors, and loosened the chains that held the prisoners. The jailer's life was in jeopardy. Lose a prisoner, lose a life – his own. Rather than face the humiliation of a public execution, the jailer drew his own sword, ready to commit suicide. But Paul's voice from the impenetrable darkness stopped him: "Do yourself no harm, for we are all here!" (Acts 16:28 NASB). What a stunning revelation! The jailer about to die by his own hand learned in that instant that men of honor and courage were in his prison. Such men must be innocent of the charges placed against them. Such men must proclaim the truth. Didn't he just hear them singing? Such men must worship the one true God.

Calling for a torch, the jailer brought Paul and Silas from the darkness of the dungeon into the light. He was eager for a glimmer of Light himself to illuminate the darkness of the despair he had just experienced. Paul and Silas gave him that Light – the Light of salvation. Humbly, the jailer washed and medicated their wounded backs and was baptized, as were the members of his household.

The next morning, perhaps ashamed of their hasty appeasement of the riotous crowd, the city fathers sent word to the jailer to release the prisoners. However, Paul and Silas refused to leave. Paul informed them that they had beaten and imprisoned Roman citizens without first conducting a trial – an unlawful act because the rights of Roman citizens were protected. This news certainly alarmed the leadership; they were at fault. With much apology and trepidation, they escorted the two men safely from prison and requested that they leave town immediately.

Paul did not threaten the city leaders with retribution for their rash act. That was not his style; after all, he had just used the incident to convert souls to Christ. Rather, he probably wanted to protect the young church at Philippi from the persecution that might result from this event. After visiting briefly with the Christians at Lydia's house, he and Silas traveled on toward Thessalonica, leaving behind Timothy and Luke to evangelize the city of Philippi further and to strengthen the infant church.

Other Visits

Paul's first trip to Philippi in approximately A.D. 50 was followed by other visits. During his third missionary journey in Acts 20, Paul traveled to Macedonia. He spent what may have been a lengthy time visiting and encouraging the churches there, which, of course, would have included Philippi. He then went on to Greece where he only stayed three months because the Jews stirred up a plot against him. Again using the Via Egnatia, he returned to Philippi where he and Luke, whose presence is indicated again by the use of first person narrative, stayed a week before sailing to Troas to join the other disciples delivering gifts for disaster relief in Judea (Acts 20:1-6; 2 Corinthians 2:12-13; 8:1-6).

The book of Acts ends with the two-year house arrest of Paul in Rome. During this time he wrote letters in which he expressed his anticipation of a release from imprisonment and a return visit to the churches where he had preached (Philippians 2:24.) It is highly likely that he was released (historical writings from Clement and Eusebius affirm it) and that he did visit Philippi again. Through events alluded to in Paul's letters and the construction of a probable timeline, many scholars believe that Paul made a fourth missionary trip after the closing of the Acts 28 narrative. For example, in 1 Timothy 1:3, Paul refers to a visit to Macedonia that is not recorded in Acts; this may have been his last visit to Philippi in approximately A.D. 66.

The Letter

Paul probably wrote the letter to the Philippians in A.D. 61 while under house arrest in Rome. Basically a letter of thanks and encouragement, Philippians is short enough to read at a single sitting. In this study, you are encouraged not only to focus on the few verses being discussed in each lesson but also to read the whole letter through several times. This practice will help you gain the total message as Paul intended it. If you let it, the letter will become a message from Paul to you personally.

Another suggestion for your study of Philippians is to read several translations, perhaps a different one each time you read the book through. The New International Version is the one cited most often here, but other translations will shed light on the exact meaning of Paul's words as he was inspired to write them in that most timely and exact language of his day – Greek.

Philippians is the golden setting for sparkling gems of truth with which we should adorn our lives on a daily basis. Only then will we "shine like stars in the universe as [we] hold out the word of life" (Philippians 2:15-16 NIV).

A CLEARER FOCUS

1. On a map of the Roman Empire, trace the route of the Via Egnatia. What other cities evangelized by Paul are on or close to this route?

2. How did God prepare the way for the spread of Christianity through the government and the infrastructure of the Roman Empire? How does God prepare governments and infrastructures for us to spread His word today?

3. Although Latin was the official language in the Roman Empire, why did God choose Greek as the language for the New Testament writers to use?

4. What excuses are sometimes given by Christians for not participating in the singing in worship? Compare our excuses with the conditions of Paul and Silas' worship in prison.

ABOVE AND BEYOND

Ancient Philippi was destroyed by the Turks. However, several Internet sites feature pictures of the excavated ruins by going to www.google.com and using the image tab feature to look up Philippi, Macedonia. One of the best sites for photography and information is www.bibleplaces.com.

THE FORGET-ME-
NOTS OF THE ANGELS

Philippians 1:1-11

"Blossomed the lovely stars – the forget-me-nots of the angels."
– Henry Wadsworth Longfellow

The art of the handwritten note or letter is almost extinct. It should not be. Although it is easy and convenient to make a quick phone call or to send a pre-fab Internet card complete with bells and whistles, neither of these can compete with the thoughtfully handwritten, personal words that come from a friend or admirer. Notice the emphasis on the word *personal*. Although a card with a printed sentiment placed in a stamped envelope is better than the impersonal online variety, it still in no way compares with handwritten words from the heart of the writer, no matter how awkwardly phrased. How many mothers have cherished a scrawled, misspelled, but thoroughly sincere note written by a child, saving it with other precious mementoes?

When was the last time you actually wrote a note or letter to someone? Not a quick "thinking of you" at the bottom of a preprinted card, but a note or letter written on stationary or on a blank card saying exactly what you mean it to say? In our fast-paced, instantaneous, satellite-reflected world, doesn't it make you feel special if someone actually slows down long enough to handwrite meaningful words to you from the heart? And the wonderful advantage those written words have over spoken words is that they can be saved to be read over and over again, long after the occasion of writing has passed.

Our written words can influence lives long after we are gone. In my possession is a cedar chest full of family treasures including a letter written to my grandmother by her second husband in 1898. Although I barely remember her and was the grandchild of her third husband, I know from this letter how much this man adored and cherished her – how he longed to return to her side. I also know both of them were anguished over the miscarriage of a child, never to have one in the future. As a teenager, I read his letter. Through his loving words I saw an example of a strong, abiding marriage with a commitment to the sacred vows taken before God, broken only by his untimely death. How many times my grandmother must have read that letter in her lifetime.

Paul's letter to the Philippians is also a love letter, but of the spiritual kind. It is a thank you note to faraway Christian friends for their continued interest and loving support and an encouragement for them to continue in the faith. His written words to them can continue to influence our lives today if we open our hearts to them. By closely studying this wonderful letter, we can learn more about our own relationships: what we should do for one another and how we should treat one another.

The first eight verses, although fairly typical of the beginning words of most of Paul's letters, demonstrate some basic Christian principles of communication that we can use as we converse with others in spiritual and worldly settings.

Principle #1

Treat those with whom you communicate as equals. Never talk down to anyone. In his letters to the Macedonian churches at Philippi and Thessalonica, Paul never mentions his position as an apostle. Being an apostle, of course, was as prominent a position as an early Christian could have. Being an apostle meant that Paul actually saw Christ, that he had the authority and inspiration to speak for Him, and that he could work miracles in His name. Why did Paul find it superfluous to identify himself as an apostle to the Philippian church? The Philippians had never called into question the validity of his apostleship as had some converts in other locations. Therefore, it was not necessary for him to defend himself as an apostle-come-lately to these Christians. Furthermore, Paul was not boastful; he did not use his title of apostle to impress anyone with his superiority. Rather, he identified himself as a servant of Christ Jesus, which is key to his message of servitude later in the letter.

Brag!: The Art of Tooting Your Own Horn Without Blowing It is a book published for those trying to get ahead in the corporate world. The author, Peggy Klaus, holds seminars where clients are told to provide a "brag along" about themselves to mention in conversation. Although a job applicant must provide a résumé and be willing to talk about what he or she has accomplished, this new idea goes a step further by teaching people not only to be subtle name-droppers, but brag-droppers as well. Thankfully, many of Klaus' clients feel reluctant to brag about themselves, and one can only hope she will not convert them to this new, in-your-face practice.

When we try to impress others with either our worldly or spiritual positions, we are taking the opposite attitude to the one taught in Philippians. One of my most embarrassing moments (and rightfully so) was a time when I identified myself publicly as having received a particular award in a specially called teachers' meeting at the state department of education only to find out that every other teacher there had received the same award. Talk about a humility check! I still blush when I think about it. If we, in some way, have managed to be singled out for worldly honor or for a position of authority, our audience probably knows about it already. In fact, they may be intimidated by both our talents and our position in life. How much better it is to downplay our successes and concentrate on making others feel comfortable talking to us.

As an English teacher in a crowd of people who don't know me, I try to identify myself simply as a teacher. Nothing stifles conversation quicker than others becoming aware that they are talking to an English teacher! Instead of worrying about what is being said, they worry about their grammar. I teach my students to speak and write with more formal grammar in my classroom because I want them to feel comfortable if they are asked to communicate with a college president or dean. At the same time, I teach them to talk informally as they normally would in our local setting, especially to the elderly or to family members, such as a grandpa in his overalls on the farm. Our goal should always be to make the person with whom we are speaking comfortable and unintimidated.

Principle #2

Do recognize and give credit to the work of others. Paul includes Timothy in his salutation although the letter is actually from the heart and mind of Paul. Perhaps Timothy wrote the letter from Paul's dictation, for which Paul is giving him credit. Or Paul may have mentioned him at the beginning of the letter because he planned to send Timothy to check on the saints at Philippi in the near future (Philippians 2:19-20). In either case, he gives credit to the presence of Timothy who is at his side serving him like a son and who, of course, would also be interested in the welfare of the Philippian disciples. Similarly today, a woman might write a letter or note and include her husband's and/or children's names because their sentiments, although they are not actually writing the letter themselves, are the same as hers, and they are a family.

Paul also singles out the bishops (elders, overseers) and deacons as two groups of men who work together with the saints at Philippi. These men have the daily responsibility for the spiritual growth and work of the church. How very right it is to recognize that extra measure of responsibility they carry.

Principle #3

Make each individual feel a part of the group. A common problem in the church today is our faulty communication with the group as a whole. Sometimes the church leaders assume that because they know something, everyone else knows, too. How embarrassing and left out a member feels when he or she reads in the church bulletin about a death in the family of a fellow Christian a week or two after the fact. The modern phone tree helps overcome this problem but only if it is used expeditiously. Likewise, members need to know that others have noticed their absence, whether from an illness, a death in the family, a vacation or simply missing-in-action. If one of our children did not show up at the dinner table, wouldn't we be concerned?

In his first letter to the Corinthian church (12:14-20), Paul's analogical comparison of the church to a human body is a powerful presentation of how important it is for each individual member to function as and feel a part of the group as a whole. It is no wonder that Paul, in the first eight verses of Philippians 1, uses the word *all* five times: "To all the saints" (v. 1); "my prayers for all of you" (v. 4); "right for me to feel this way about all of you" (v. 7); "all of you share in God's grace with me" (v. 7); and "I long for all of you with the affection of Christ Jesus" (v. 8).

Principle #4

Be supportive. Paul immediately lets the Philippian saints know that he prays for them with joy and confidence (Philippians 1:4-6). Nothing we do for each other can be more supportive than a prayer offered joyfully and confidently, knowing that God will answer. James concurs with Paul when he says that the "prayer of a righteous man is powerful and effective" (James 5:16). Although we must put our faith and love for our Christian family into action by doing what we can for each other, we must never forget that the ultimate answer to life's problems is only a prayer away.

Paul's prayer for the Philippians was specific. He prayed that their love would continue to grow by leaps and bounds. How? Through the "knowledge and depth of insight" (Philippians 1:9). How we need Paul's prayer even today! Only through a thorough and prayerful study of God's Word can we mature in the wisdom needed to make good judgments about the actions we take in our daily lives. Furthermore, our ability to judge will not be limited just to what is right or wrong, but we will also be able to choose what is best among the better decisions that come our way (v. 10). The Philippians then and we today need good judgment so that we "may be pure and blameless until the day of Christ" (v. 10) and so that we will be "filled with the fruit of righteousness" (v. 11). The same fruit is mentioned in Paul's letter to the Galatians: "love, joy, peace, patience, kindness, goodness, faithfulness, gentleness and self-control" (Galatians 5:22-23). According to Christ in His most famous sermon, our righteousness must exceed that of the old law (Matthew 5:20). We must go the extra mile. Steeping ourselves in God's Word will make us better servants so that we, like Paul, may be "poured out like a drink offering" (Philippians 2:17) on the sacrifice and service of our faith.

A CLEARER FOCUS

1. Share with the class a specific written encouragement you received from a fellow Christian or another friend that has meant a lot to you (perhaps you even saved it).

2. What are practical suggestions for improving your own practice of personal letter and/or note writing?

3. What are practical suggestions for improving church-wide communication? How are we failing to communicate? What can we each do personally and collectively to improve our communication within the church?

4. How does Bible study lead to the fruit of righteousness? Explain the process.

ABOVE AND BEYOND

Send a card this week to a fellow Christian thanking him/her for being a good example of service to the Lord for you personally.

YE QUENCHLESS STARS!

Philippians 1:12-14

"Ye quenchless stars! so eloquently bright,
Untroubled sentries of the shadowy night."
– Robert Montgomery

After greeting the Philippians, Paul tells them about the circumstances in which he finds himself. He is imprisoned, not for any crime he has committed, but for preaching the gospel of Jesus Christ. Most scholars believe this is the occasion of his house arrest in Rome, mentioned in the closing verses of Acts. He is guarded at all times by at least one of Caesar's palace guards, who exchange watches around the clock.

This was not Paul's first imprisonment. He experienced several others and a multitude of tribulations during his years as a servant of Christ, including at least eight beatings (five by Jews and three by Romans), a stoning, shipwrecks and a complete day and night lost at sea. In his travels, he was tormented by sleeplessness, hunger, thirst, hypothermia and harrowing escapes from death (2 Corinthians 11:23-27).

From our viewpoint, Paul could be called a man of constant sorrow. His life brings us to that age-old question asked by Job: Why do bad things happen to good people? No one could have been more dedicated, more deeply spiritual, more filled with joy than Paul, and yet he suffered as none of us have suffered. Shouldn't God have kept Paul safe from so much persecution? Shouldn't He shield us, too, from harm and temptation? We look around us at worldly people who make no attempt to follow the paths of righteousness, who never darken the door of a church, and yet everything seems to go right for them. They get the plum job, drive a Mercedes, live in a three-story mansion, never get sick, and their kids get in the best universities. Meanwhile, many Christians struggle to pay the bills, drive a second-hand clunker, live in a cookie-cutter house, get cancer, and go in debt to send their kids to a Christian college. What's wrong with this picture?

The problem is that we are looking in the wrong end of the telescope. Our values should not be the values the world espouses. God never promised the Christian protection from the slings and arrows of outrageous fortune. We are human, living in a human world, where we are subject to the same illnesses, accidents and angst as our worldly neighbors. If we had some special protection from suffering, the world would be clamoring to become Christians just to escape the trials of life, not because of faith in Jesus Christ. The promises of God are summed up most aptly by Annie Johnson Flint in her poem "What God Hath Promised" (Swindoll 235):

> God hath not promised
> Skies always blue
> Flower-strewn pathways
> All our lives through;
>
> God hath not promised
> Sun without rain
> Joy without sorrow,
> Peace without pain.
>
> But God hath promised
> Strength for the day
> Rest for the labor
> Light for the way;

Grace for the trials
Help from above
Unfailing sympathy
Undying love.

Two of God's special promises to Christians stand out above the rest: He will not allow us to be tempted more than we can stand (1 Corinthians 10:13); and if we persevere we will receive "the crown of life" (Revelation 2:10) and have a home with Him in heaven where there will be "no more death or mourning or crying or pain" (21:4).

So, the question remains: Why do bad things happen to good people? Paul's life and God's Word give us several answers.

Through Adversity ...

• ... *the Christian is strengthened.* Have you ever grown tomato plants from seed in a hotbed, anticipating the day you can transplant those tender seedlings to the garden where they will produce luscious homegrown fruit? What happens to those spindly little plants if you take them directly from the hothouse to the garden? Right – no tomatoes, dead plant! First, you must place the plant outdoors in a sheltered place where its resistance to a little wind will help it grow strong. Then, you gradually put it in full sun. What you are doing to that young plant is disciplining or training it for the heat of the sun and the strength of the wind.

God disciplines His children in the same way (Hebrews 12:7). Without the buffeting of life's gales, we would be unable to stand firm in the faith. If we were not disciplined, God would not have shown His love for us because all proper discipline stems from love (v. 6), and God is love (1 John 4:8). Discipline is a necessary and vital part of maturing. We want that tomato plant to grow and mature so it will produce fruit; God wants His children to grow and mature so they will produce fruit. Although discipline is never pleasant at the time, it will produce "a harvest of righteousness and peace for those who have been trained by it" (Hebrews 12:11). Paul sums it all up later in Philippians when he says, "I can do everything through him who gives me strength" (4:13).

• ... *we gain the ability to empathize.* When a sister in Christ loses her young child to cancer, I can sympathize, but I can't empathize no

25

matter how hard I try. Sympathy is "a feeling or expression of sorrow for the distress of another; compassion; commiseration." Empathy is "understanding so intimate that the feelings, thoughts, and motives of one are readily comprehended by another" (*American Heritage Dictionary*). Only if I have walked a mile in her shoes can I even come close to understanding the pain and anguish that young mother is feeling. Although none of us want to suffer, it is inevitable that we will – some more than others. A Christian must take that tragedy or loss and use it to empathize with others who face the same experience.

Amy is a 30-year-old, recently pinned nurse in our church. At the age of 25, she lost her husband to leukemia and was left with three small children, all under school age. She spent many torturous weeks sitting by her husband's bedside in the ward for bone marrow transplants at Vanderbilt Hospital in Nashville, Tenn., watching him suffer until this last-ditch treatment failed. She had married young, had little education, and had never been independent. God provided her with a new husband and father to her children from among our number, a bachelor just a few years older than she. He encouraged her to go back to school while he provided stability for her children through his loving discipline. Amy's confidence and abilities grew, and today she has given her life a new purpose by working as a nurse in the same ward where she watched her first husband die. Talk about the ability to empathize! Amy changed tragedy to triumph.

Paul, too, truly understood empathy. He suffered a thorn in the flesh that God refused to remove (2 Corinthians 12:7-9), and he had spent his early years persecuting Christians with the same zeal that he later used to promote Christ. In 2 Corinthians 11:29 he says, "Who is weak, and I do not feel weak? Who is led into sin, and I do not inwardly burn?" We, too, may have suffered adversity. And most certainly, we, too, have sinned. Therefore, like Paul, we should be able to empathize with our Christian brothers and sisters as they face the trials and temptations of this life.

• *... we learn to depend on God.* "Your enemy the devil prowls around like a roaring lion looking for someone to devour" (1 Peter 5:8), and his favorite meal is a Christian. With every temptation God provides a way of escape (1 Corinthians 10:13); all we need to do is ask for His guidance. If we search His Word diligently and let it penetrate our hearts, He will direct our steps. As the psalmist said, "Your word is a lamp to my feet and a light for my path" (Psalm 119:105).

God is "the God of all comfort, who comforts us in all our troubles" (2 Corinthians 1:3-4). Putting our problems and worries in God's hands, confident that He is in charge of our lives, is the ultimate blessing for the Christian. As V. Raymond Edman says, "I am here (1) by God's appointment (2) in his keeping (3) under his training (4) for his time" (Swindoll 244). The catch phrase of the day is "Let go, and let God." Although it sounds trite, it is true. The only way to face adversity is to submit completely and turn our lives over to Him.

• ... *we can be a shining example for others.* In Philippians 1:13-14, Paul tells how he used his imprisonment in Rome to further the cause of Christ. He continued to teach and preach, converting many of the soldiers who guarded him, as well as servants and other workers in Caesar's household. His perseverance and dedication to Christ served as an example to other Christians in the area, giving them the courage to speak for Christ as well.

"You are the light of the world" (Matthew 5:14a). I have previously related the story of one of the "stars" in my Christian family – Amy, the nurse. A second star is Mrs. Betty, probably one of the most deeply spiritual women I have ever known. When she was diagnosed with a rare degenerative condition known as Shy-Drager syndrome several years ago, she was told that she had, at best, five years to live. She explained to our Wednesday night ladies class exactly what would be happening to her: a gradual onset of atrophy in her muscles and organs until her body would ultimately shut down and death would occur.

Never one to complain about her lot in life, she did not pray or ask us to pray for a cure, but rather for her to use this experience as an example of accepting the vicissitudes of life with full faith in the Lord and her home with Him in Heaven. At first, it was difficult to believe she was so ill, but gradually her body denied her the ability to walk, and her loving husband, Ed, brought her to church in a wheelchair. Finally, even that was impossible, but through it all she smiled, called everyone "darling," and let her light shine. She left this life to be with her Lord without ever murmuring a complaint, and God, at Mrs. Betty's request, provided Ed with a second loving wife, a widowed friend of hers in our church family. As with Amy, Mrs. Betty turned tragedy to triumph and was a shining example of God's grace and mercy working through adversity.

From a Different View

The Christian must rejoice in adversity as Paul rejoiced. Sometimes our lives seem so darkened by the storms of life that it is difficult for us to remember that above the clouds the sun is shining brightly. We must step outside ourselves, look through God's end of the telescope, and see the big picture from His point of view, remembering that He is in control and that "all things work together for good to them that love God, to them who are the called according to his purpose" (Romans 8:28 KJV).

A CLEARER FOCUS

1. In your own words, explain the difference between *sympathy* and *empathy*.

2. What adversities have you experienced that gave you opportunities to empathize with others?

3. Name some national organizations based on empathy.

4. What are some negative outcomes of adversity? What are some positive outcomes of adversity? What determines the outcome?

ABOVE AND BEYOND

Pray about the adversities you have experienced. Ask God to help you find the purpose and meaning in them so that He can use you as a light to others.

4

STARS, HIDE YOUR FIRES

Philippians 1:15-30

"Stars, hide your fires;
Let not light see my black and deep desires."
– William Shakespeare

William Shakespeare's tragic play *Macbeth* explores hypocrisy. Early in the drama, Lady Macbeth gives her husband advice about how to hide his true motives: "Look like the innocent flower, / But be the serpent under 't" (1.5.65-66). On his way to kill King Duncan, Macbeth shows he has learned his lesson well: "False face must hide what the false heart doth know" (1.7.81). Ironically, King Duncan, while speaking of another traitor, has already observed, "There's no art / To find the mind's construction in the face" (1.4.13-14). Similarly, we often fail to recognize the true motives of others by taking them at face value. More importantly, we sometimes deceive even ourselves about our own motives.

Some who were preaching and teaching while Paul was in prison in Rome were doing so from false motives. The gospel that they preached was sound, but their reasons for preaching it involved jealousy, rivalry and selfish ambition (Philippians 1:15-17). Some even wanted to stir up trouble for Paul. This perhaps was the cruelest form of adversity to come from his imprisonment – enmity and spite from other preachers.

Unfortunately, jealousy and rivalry between preachers and teachers can still occur today in the Lord's church. The humility we will study in depth in Philippians 2 is hard to come by when preachers jockey for positions of eminence and renown and try to get in the last word. Sometimes hairs are split as watchdogs scrutinize every phrase and word choice of the latest popular preacher with little concern for the context. Sometimes churches split. We are just as guilty today of jealousy and rivalry, causing mental anguish to us and our Christian brothers and sisters. Despite his ill-use by others, Paul rejoiced that the gospel was being preached by both those whose hearts were pure and even by those whose hearts were impure (Philippians 1:18). Hopefully, we can emulate Paul's attitude and simply rejoice in the fact that the Lord is preached. After all, we are but earthen vessels; only God knows the content of the heart of others.

We should, however, know our own hearts. Objectivity is the key. Sometimes we lie to ourselves without realizing that we are doing so. For example, why do we go to worship? Why are we members of the congregation we now attend? Why do we teach a children's Bible class? In other words, what are our motives for worshiping and working for the Lord? Do we have a hidden agenda?

We must look at ourselves without rose-colored glasses and see ourselves for what we truly are: sinful creatures dependent on the grace of God. Here are some questions that demand an honest answer.

• Am I as eager to attend worship as I am to attend a sporting event, concert or movie?

• Am I a member of this church because I find the worship more entertaining and exciting than other churches?

• Am I more worried about the external aspects of worship than I am about my internal participation?

• Do I participate in one of the ministries of the church? Or do I just attend worship?

Be honest! There are times when we all have to make ourselves go to worship. We are only human, and all of us experience those low moments when the recliner looks more comfortable to our tired minds and bodies than the church pew. Have you ever nodded off during a sermon? Eutychus did (Acts 20:7-9). Perhaps he stayed up too late the night before as we often do. We have a problem, though, if we find that our low moments always occur on Sundays and Wednesday nights. These occasions should be the high points in our weekly schedule.

The Entertainment Factor

We all want to be entertained. In fact, we are the entertainment generation. As a child, the movie theater was my baby-sitter. I also hunted lions and tigers with a stick spear in the field next door and cooked their meat on my concrete-block stove. Today, the baby-sitting is done at home with the television and/or a DVD player featuring digital surround sound. Why should children play outside in the heat and use their imaginations when they have fast-paced, exciting video games at the flick of a thumb? From childhood on, our entire lives are filled with entertainment with little or no effort on our part. No wonder we think of ourselves as the audience at church! No wonder we want to be entertained in worship!

I am appalled by a TV commercial showing a family dressed for recreation watching a rock band on stage with the message that this is not what it appears to be, but instead a new, exciting form of worship. Aren't we confusing things a little here? Dan Chambers, in his book *Showtime! Worship in the Age of Show Business,* quotes from church brochures that advertise "State of the art video, graphics, drama in comfortable theater seats," and "you'll love our free coffee, soft drinks and doughnuts" (28). Chambers also quotes John MacArthur: "Instead of a pulpit, the focus is a stage. Churches are hiring full-time media specialists, programming consultants, stage directors, drama coaches, special-effects experts, and choreographers" (32). Although many wonderful electronic inventions of our modern age are useful aids to biblical worship, they must not be substituted for the real purpose of our coming together. After all, whom is worship for?

Actually, we are the performers and God is the audience. Our "performance" should not be hypocritical (*hypocrite* in Greek means actor), but as worshipers, we "must worship in spirit and in truth" (John 4:24). It does not matter if our singing – the one part of worship in which we women may verbalize our thoughts – is beautiful or pleasing to our own ears. We must sing with the spirit and the understanding (1 Corinthians 14:15). We must let the words "teach and admonish" us (Colossians 3:16). We must perform the act of worship.

The Heart of the Matter

Sometimes we are too caught up in the external, worldly aspects of worship. Ever had these thoughts, or similar ones, during worship?

> Only one man at the front has on a shirt and tie. And why does Tony stand with his feet sprattled out like an oil derrick? Jeff needs to speak up – the microphone is squealing again. Lonnie needs to adjust the air conditioning – it's too cold in here for the old folks. Why does Charles have to sit behind me and sing off key? Little Luke surely is cute repeating "Amen" after all the prayers. I wish someone would take that squalling brat in the back out to the nursery. Some of the teens are talking again and not paying attention to the lesson. We surely do need new carpet in here. Wonder who did that flower arrangement? Mrs. Idell has a new dress – looks pretty on her. Somebody misspelled the words on Powerpoint again – I wish they'd use spell-check. I hope the preacher isn't wound up today and we get out in time to beat the Baptists to Shoney's.

Sound familiar? It is so easy to let the worldly part of our nature intrude on the spiritual. We must wage a constant battle to keep our focus on what is truly important in our worship of God. It doesn't matter if we are having a bad hair day. Or if the baby just spit up on our shoulder. Or if our husband's tie doesn't match his suit. Or if we forgot and wore our knee-highs with a split skirt. It doesn't matter to God if we are in picked double-knit or cashmere. God cares what we bring to Him inside – hopefully, a humble and contrite heart opened willingly to praise Him and be filled with His Word. Remember what God told Samuel: "The Lord does not look at the things man looks at. Man looks at the outward appearance, but the Lord looks at the heart" (1 Samuel 16:7).

It is amazing to me that two murderers – one in the Old Testament, the other in the New – had their hearts so attuned to God. We think of murder as a most heinous crime. Yet David, who ordered Uriah murdered to cover up his sin of adultery, was called "a man after [God's] own heart" (1 Samuel 13:14). And, Saul, later renamed Paul, held the coats of those who stoned Stephen, aiding and abetting the crime, and then went on to hunt down more Christians to execute. Why would Christ appear to such a man on the road to Damascus? As with David's, God could see Saul's heart. David immediately and contritely responded to the prophet Nathan with "I have sinned against the Lord" (2 Samuel 12:13) and then wrote his heart-wrenching, confessional prayer in Psalm 51. Saul immediately responded with "What shall I do, Lord?" (Acts 22:10; 9:1-19), waited sightlessly for three days for the answer, and then accepted his Savior in baptism. Despite their sinful actions and their wrong motives, both men readily accepted personal responsibility for their sins with humble and contrite hearts. Both men were ready and willing to have a change of heart.

We, too, must be honest with ourselves and God. We, too, must let God work in our hearts. Otherwise, when we worship, we will be like the Pharisees so aptly described by Christ in Matthew 23:25-26: "You clean the outside of the cup and dish, but inside they are full of greed and self-indulgence. Blind Pharisee! First clean the inside of the cup and dish, and then the outside also will be clean."

How do we clean the dregs of sinful motives from our hearts? We must step back from our daily planners and look at the wall calendar of our lives. If all we ever do is schedule worship on Sundays and Wednesday nights, we have a heart problem. In fact, if we only worship God publicly and never privately, we have a heart problem. If we only open our Bibles at church and never at home, we have a heart problem. If we only pray when a public prayer is led, we have a heart problem. Our daily lives must be Christ-centered – not just Sundays, but every day of the week.

Many people think that all there is to Christianity is attending worship. Perhaps we have been misled by that misnomer "worship service." We talk about the services of the church, but the true services of the church are carried out on Monday, Tuesday, Wednesday, Thursday, Friday, Saturday and Sunday. Paul says in Philippians 1:21-22, "For to me, to live is Christ and to die is gain. If I am to go on living in the body, this will mean fruitful labor for me." Fruitful labor for Christ is expected of all of us. On Sundays, for an hour or two, we lay our work aside and commune with God in worship – no labor involved!

Every church has ministries that fit the varied talents of its members. Find your niche. Then fill it. It doesn't have to be a ministry with a name like "benevolence" or "rest home services" or "visitation" or "nursery care." Are you good with children? Some young mother is struggling to care for her little ones. Sit near her in worship and help her out by becoming a surrogate grandmother. Become her favorite free baby sitter while she goes to the grocery store or to get her hair done. Or adopt an elderly person as your own surrogate grandmother. Go sit with her on her front porch and visit. Read to her from the Bible. Listen to her wisdom, gleaned from years of living. What you choose as your personal ministry is not important; the important thing is that you choose to minister for Christ.

How will you know that you are being successful? You will bear fruit for Christ. He says, "I am the vine; you are the branches. If a man remains in me and I in him, he will bear much fruit" (John 15:5). You will win others to Christ by your teaching and your good works. No longer will you have to hide behind the glitter of hypocrisy, but your star will shine from the purity of your heart and the internal glow of Christ living in you.

A CLEARER FOCUS

1. What are some wrong reasons for which a person might choose to worship with a particular congregation?

2. Statistics show that many congregations lose some members and gain others every time a new preacher is hired. Why do you think this happens? Is it good to choose a congregation because of a preacher?

3. How can people do right with wrong motives today? Is God pleased with the results?

4. Should we continue our worship and work for the Lord when our motives are not right? Why or why not?

ABOVE AND BEYOND

• If you are not involved in a ministry, choose a good work and become involved. Tell the eldership what you would like to do as your part in the Lord's work. Talk about the work with fellow Christians and tell them your intentions. Be supportive of their work and let them be supportive of yours.

• Commit to memory Philippians 1:21.

For too me to live is Christ, and to die is gain.

5

HARMONY OF THE STARS

Philippians 2:1-4

"Where wast thou when I laid the foundations of the earth? declare, if thou hast understanding. Who hath laid the measures thereof, if though knowest? ... or who laid the corner stone thereof; When the morning stars sang together, and all the sons of God shouted for joy?" (Job 38:4-7 KJV).

The Preacher in the ancient book of Ecclesiastes truly understood the human need for companionship. Sometimes our very survival depends on the strength found in a unified effort:

> Two are better than one, because they have a good return for their work: If one falls down, his friend can help him up. But pity the man who falls and has no one to help him up! Also, if two lie down together, they will keep warm. But how can one keep warm alone? Though one may be over-powered, two can defend themselves. A cord of three strands is not quickly broken (Ecclesiastes 4:9-12).

God never intended for man to be alone to face the adversities of life; for this reason He instituted marriage and made Adam a helper (Genesis 2:18). With the addition of God as the third strand of any marital relationship, we have the ultimate strength for perseverance. Similarly, God sent His Son to establish the church. Christ says that "where two or three come together in my name, there am I with them" (Matthew 18:20). The church, with Christ as its Head, provides each member with the strength for perseverance. Again, "A cord of three strands is not quickly broken."

Compare the strength of one or two strands with that of many strands. A thread will break, but woven fabric is hard to tear. Twine will hold a package, but a twisted rope is needed to confine a calf. And what about the strength of the cables – 36½ inches in diameter – holding up the Golden Gate Bridge in San Francisco Bay? There is strength in numbers. It all depends on the individual strength of each separate strand and the quality of the weave. Paul addresses these two key elements in the heart of his message to the Philippian church.

The Strength of the Individual

A group is only as strong as the individuals who make up that group. For that reason, Paul begins his plea for unity in Philippians 2 with the individual. He reminds us, first of all, of our personal source of strength as recipients of encouragement, love and fellowship.

• *We have the encouragement that comes from being united with Christ.* How? When we are baptized, we put Him on and become a child of God: "You are all sons of God through faith in Christ Jesus, for all of you who were baptized into Christ have clothed yourself with Christ" (Galatians 3:26-27). We no longer live; Christ lives in us: "I have been crucified with Christ and I no longer live, but Christ lives in me. The life I live in the body, I live by faith in the Son of God, who loved me and gave himself for me" (2:20). Our encouragement comes from the fact that we are no longer condemned by our sin "because through Christ Jesus the law of the Spirit of life set [us] free from the law of sin and death" (Romans 8:1-2). We can say with Paul in Philippians 1:21, "For to me, to live is Christ and to die is gain," because we know that no matter what persecutions or suffering may come our way,

in the end we will live with Christ in heaven. What an encouragement that is for us to live for Him each day!

• *We have the comfort of His love.* John 3:16 tells us how much God
loves us, a message reiterated emphatically by the same writer in
1 John 3:1: "How great is the love the Father has lavished on us, that
we should be called children of God! And that is what we are!" The
word translated in the New International Version as "lavished" tells the
whole story. We are not loved a little; we are loved a lot! God's love is
not just a token gift such as we might give a mere acquaintance; it is
a gift given to a favored child, effusive in its abundance. No matter what
happens, "neither death nor life, neither angels nor demons, neither the
present nor the future, nor any powers, neither height nor depth, nor
anything else in all creation, will be able to separate us from the love
of God that is in Christ Jesus our Lord" (Romans 8:38-39). If you are
a mother, you know how much you love your children. Multiply that
love by infinity and you will find the love of God is unfathomable!

• *We have "fellowship together in the Spirit"* (Philippians 2:1 NEW
LIVING BIBLE). How important it is for each of us to pierce our hearts
daily with "the sword of the Spirit, which is the word of God" (Ephesians
6:17), for it "is living and active. Sharper than any double-edged sword,
it penetrates even to dividing soul and spirit, joints and marrow; it judges
the thoughts and attitudes of the heart" (Hebrews 4:12). At the same time,
however, we must also continue in fellowship with other spiritually mind-
ed people. That is why Christians are exhorted to "consider how we may
spur one another on toward love and good deeds. Let us not give up meeting together, as some are in the habit of doing, but let us encourage one
another" (10:24-25). We are unified as an army of God, and we support each other with our sword of truth in heart and hand.

All three of these blessings in Christ are mentioned together in Paul's
prayer for the Corinthian brethren at the closing of his second letter:
"May the grace of the Lord Jesus Christ, and the love of God, and the
fellowship of the Holy Spirit be with you all" (13:14). Because we are
so lavished with encouragement, love and fellowship, we, in turn, must
rightfully be filled with tenderness and compassion toward others
(Philippians 2:1). John says in 1 John 3:16-19:

This is how we know what love is: Jesus Christ laid down
his life for us. And we ought to lay down our lives for our
brothers. If anyone has material possessions and sees his
brother in need but has no pity on him, how can the love
of God be in him? Dear children, let us not love with words
or tongue but with actions and in truth. This then is how we
know that we belong to the truth, and how we set our hearts
at rest in his presence.

Paul told the Colossians to "clothe yourselves with compassion, kindness, humility, gentleness and patience" (3:12). These virtues will man-
ifest our relationships with God, Christ and the Holy Spirit and demonstrate our willingness to be woven into the fabric of the church "to keep
the unity of the Spirit through the bond of peace" (Ephesians 4:3).

The Strength of the Weave

Human nature is selfish: I want what I want, and I want it now! We
come into the world with this demand. We cry, and someone feeds us
when we are hungry; someone rocks us when we are sleepy; and someone changes our diaper when we are uncomfortably wet. As we grow,
our parents try to civilize us. They don't respond quite so quickly to
our needs, and we learn to wait awhile. Civilizing a child means teaching her that other people in the world also have needs that have to be
met – maybe before her own! At a later age, in worship and in school,
we train that same child to put the good of the group ahead of her own
desires – disturbing the peace is frowned upon!

Human nature is also factious. We tend to group ourselves according to common interests and beliefs. We enjoy being around people
who are cut from the same cloth. Sometimes, however, we join a particular group because we aren't civilized as well as our parents thought
– we still want our egos stroked! Sometimes we unravel ourselves from
a group that refuses to see things our way. The immaturity of selfish-
ness again rears its ugly head!

Through inspiration from the Master Weaver, Paul defines the warp
and woof that constitute the united strength of the fabric of the church
in Philippians 2:2.

• *Be like-minded.* The Corinthian church had a problem with this unifying attribute (1 Corinthians 1:11-15). They were quarreling over whom to follow: Apollos? Peter? Paul? Or Christ? In other words, they had become preacher-followers. How many times this happens within the Lord's church! We say, "Well, my preacher says ..." or "I don't like that preacher because ... ." Sometimes, we even leave our local congregation to follow our favorite preacher to another congregation. Paul was thankful on this occasion that he had personally baptized only Crispus and Gaius, and he admonished the Corinthians to have "no divisions" (v. 10). The body of Christ should never be divided.

Being like-minded does not mean we have to agree on every little matter – only on matters of faith. If we keep the attitude of considering others and their interests before ourselves (Philippians 2:3-4), the little matters will remain exactly what they are – little matters of no matter. Actually, if we are busy, we will have little time to complain or be bothered with differences of opinion. We will have no time to be busybodies. We need to "work out [our] salvation with fear and trembling" (Philippians 2:12) and make it our "ambition to lead a quiet life, to mind [our] own business and to work with [our] hands" (1 Thessalonians 4:11). This individuality in no way weakens the unity of the group but rather strengthens it because "where the Spirit of the Lord is, there is freedom" (2 Corinthians 3:17). At the same time, we must not use our freedom to indulge in fleshly appetites but rather to "serve one another in love" (Galatians 5:13). If we truly put others before ourselves, we can enjoy the blessings of both individual freedom and church unity at the same time.

• *Have the same love.* True love prefers others over self. What better words to describe the attributes of Christian love than the famous love chapter (1 Corinthians 13): not envious, not boastful, not proud, not rude, not selfish, not easily angered; but patient, kind, protective, trusting, hopeful, forgiving, persevering, steadfast. Love supersedes all other gifts and all other virtues. It is the ultimate godlike virtue because "God is love" (1 John 4:8).

Love is active. It demonstrates itself, not through words, but through deeds. In fact, in our daily lives we have trivialized the words *I love you*. We throw them in at the end of every phone conversation and make them a habitual substitution for "good-bye," then mistreat, and some-times abuse, the very person to whom we have said, "I love you." The old saying "I'd rather see a sermon any day than hear one" goes for love as well: I'd rather see love in action than hear a meaningless "I love you." Empty words are like dead leaves to be whisked away on the first stormy day, but true love has strong and abiding roots that nour-ish and give life to the blossoming tree. So it is with the acts of love that support and nourish other Christians as they bear fruit for Christ, making the word *love* meaningful.

• *Be one in spirit and purpose.* Why are we here? Is everything "mean-ingless, a chasing after the wind?" (Ecclesiastes 1:14; 2:11). If it is, we do not understand that our purpose on earth is to fear God and "keep his commandments, for this is the whole duty of man" (12:13). Christ puts it this way: "But seek first his kingdom and his righteousness, and all these things will be given to you as well" (Matthew 6:33). He also gives us, along with His disciples, a charge – a purpose – in the Great Commission: "Go into all the world and preach the good news to all cre-ation. Whoever believes and is baptized will be saved, but whoever does not believe will be condemned" (Mark 16:15-16). We must never forget that the primary purpose of the church is to seek and save the lost.

Although bringing the world to Christ is the primary purpose of the unified efforts of the church as a whole, being a member of that unified whole does not dismiss me from my personal mission to teach others. Although tritely stated, it is true that " 'Go ye' (KJV) means go me." Each individual member must take responsibility for her own op-portunities to evangelize in her circle of worldly acquaintances. Although we share a part in the salvation of others through teaching in our Bible school classes and VBS, through our contributions to mission work, and through rearing our own children in Christ – all necessary and vital to the Lord's work – these activities are much like fishing in a fish bowl. Outside the protective glass of our Christian community is a vast ocean of opportunities, and if we are anchored in Christ we can weath-er the storms of criticism or ridicule that may come our way when we reach out to those beyond the safety of our comfortable, air-condi-tioned, pew-lined world. I am so touched by the lyrics of the hymn "Must I Go, and Empty-Handed?" by C.C. Luther: " 'Must I go, and empty-handed?' Must I meet my Savior so? Not one soul with which to greet Him; Must I empty-handed go?" (Wiegand 437).

To be like-minded, to have the same love, and to be one in spirit and purpose, we must first be humble, considering others better than ourselves. We must look to their interests as well as our own (Philippians 2:3-4). Romans 12:9-16 is a companion passage to Philippians 2:1-4:

> Love must be sincere. Hate what is evil; cling to what is good. Be devoted to one another in brotherly love. Honor one another above yourselves. Never be lacking in zeal, but keep your spiritual fervor, serving the Lord. Be joyful in hope, patient in affliction, faithful in prayer. Share with God's people who are in need. Practice hospitality. Bless those who persecute you; bless and do not curse. Rejoice with those who rejoice; mourn with those who mourn. Live in harmony with one another. Do not be proud, but be willing to associate with people of low position. Do not be conceited.

If we live according to these standards, the quality of the cloth we weave through our unity with our Christian family will be more precious and durable than any of the purple and fine linen sold by Lydia in Philippi. Its purple will never fade, providing an everlasting backdrop in which we will shine like stars in the universe.

A CLEARER FOCUS

1. We talk about strength in numbers. How can unity be hindered by size in a congregation with thousands of members? How can unity be promoted in such a large group?

2. In the small community or rural church, what can hinder unity of the membership? How can unity be promoted in the smaller congregation?

3. How unified is your congregation? What are its strengths? What are its weaknesses? What suggestions would you make to the elders to improve the unity of the membership?

4. What are some matters about which we can agree to disagree? What are some matters about which there can be no disagreement?

5. What obstacles keep us from evangelizing those outside the church? How can we overcome these obstacles?

ABOVE AND BEYOND

• Make a Bible bookmark with a Christian friend. Take three strands of two colors (red and white work well) of thin (⅛-inch) flat braid and one strand of gold braid. Cut to approximately 8 inches in length and tie together at one end. While one person holds the strands by the knot, the other plaits them together forming a braid of three strands. Tie off the other end. Exchange positions and make a second bookmark. Keep them in your Bibles to remind you of how keeping God in your relationship makes it strong.

• Commit to memory Philippians 2:1-4.

6

SUN OF MY SOUL

Philippians 2:5-11

"Sun of my soul, Thou Saviour dear,
It is not night if Thou be near."
– John Keble

I magine you are the most powerful leader on earth – probably the president of the United States. Imagine you are also the richest woman on earth, richer than Oprah. Imagine that you live in the grand palace of Louis XVI, with a villa on the Riviera and a penthouse atop Donald Trump's finest hotel. Imagine yourself surrounded by servants to see to your every need. Then imagine you voluntarily give it all away to charity to become homeless in the ghettos of Chicago. Not even in an infinitesimal way would you have given up what Christ gave up for you.

What a sacrifice His was! We usually speak only in terms of His death on the cross as an atonement for our sins, but His sacrifice was much more than that. Just look at what He left behind. In earthly terms, there is no parallel to Christ's sacrifice.

Christ existed as the Son of God before time began. He was "with God" and "was God" (John 1:1). By Him "all things were created:

things in heaven and on earth, visible and invisible, whether thrones or powers or rulers or authorities; all things were created by him and for him" (Colossians 1:16). However, He did not choose to hold on to the power and majesty of His position as part of the Godhead, but by His own choice, He "emptied himself" and gave it all up to become human and suffer the infirmities and weaknesses of the human condition. He swapped the infinite for the finite, the eternal for the ephemeral, the glories of Heaven for the grimness of the cross. "[T]hough he was rich, ... he became poor, so that [we] through his poverty might become rich" (2 Corinthians 8:9). He became Immanuel, truly, "God with us" (Matthew 1:23).

Understanding what Jesus Christ gave up to become one of us places the temptations of the devil in perspective. Today Satan tempts us to deny our spirituality, but he tempted Christ to deny His humanity. After Christ was baptized and the voice of God proclaimed, "This is my Son, whom I love; with him I am well pleased" (Matthew 3:17), Christ fasted 40 days and nights in the wilderness. Being human, He was hungry. Perhaps for the first time in His life, He was truly weak and famished. Satan wanted nothing more than to entice Him to give up on His plan of being the Word in the flesh (John 1:14). If he could just appeal to Christ to forsake this notion of sacrificing Himself for mankind, he could thwart the salvation of all our souls. After all, Christ had voluntarily given up all His power; He could just as easily volunteer to go back where He came from. (Or to the devil!) So Satan asked Him to show off His deity by using His powers to make bread from rocks to satisfy His hunger and by jumping off a roof to prove that God wouldn't let Him be injured. Satan even went so far as to put his own kingdom on the line if Jesus would just change His allegiance (Matthew 4:1-11). The heavenly power and glory that Christ gave up made these temptations even more attractive. It was an appeal to His ego. Surely He was "tempted in every way, just as we are – yet was without sin" (Hebrews 4:15).

With all the glorified art of Michelangelo and Raphael (halos, white skin, long effeminate curls, attending angels), it is difficult to imagine Jesus Christ living like an ordinary Jewish man, but He did. He got hungry, and when He did, He ate with sinners (Matthew 9:9-13). He grew tired, and when He did, He lay in a boat and slept (8:24). He helped celebrate a wedding (John 2:1-11), He loved the company of children (Matthew 19:13-14), He cried with His friends when their brother died (John 11:33-35), and having worked as a carpenter, He was strong enough to wield a whip and drive the greedy moneychangers from the temple (2:13-16). He also had His quiet moments alone communing with His heavenly Father (Mark 6:46). And He was so anguished in Gethsemene before His death that His sweat dropped like blood on the ground (Luke 22:44). All the sensations and emotions that we experience, Jesus experienced – without sin.

Christ willingly "made himself nothing, taking the very nature of a servant" (Philippians 2:7). In John 10:17-18, He said, "I lay down my life – only to take it up again. No one takes it from me, but I lay it down of my own accord." He willingly submitted to the most cruel punishment devised for criminals – death on a cross. The nails ripped agonizingly through the flesh in His hands and His feet; the thorns pierced the tender skin at His temples; His throat and mouth ached with dryness when He cried, "I thirst." His death was not the more humane beheading by sword reserved for Roman citizens – a death such as Paul probably experienced years later (Clarke 1033) – but a slow, tortuous, inhumane, public execution. Not only was this type of death cruel, but it was the most shameful as well because, according to Jewish law, "anyone who is hung on a tree is under God's curse" (Deuteronomy 21:23). Through this cruel and shameful death, we are given life, for "God made him who had no sin to be sin for us, so that in him we might become the righteousness of God" (2 Corinthians 5:21). What a sacrifice! What a servant!

The Same Attitude

The key scripture in our Philippians focus is 2:5: "Your attitude should be the same as that of Christ Jesus." Although we can never attain a sinless state and although we can never sacrifice as much as He did, we are to have the mind of Christ – a voluntary submission to God and servitude to others. In Christ's own words: " 'Love the Lord your God with all your heart and with all your soul and with all your mind.' This is the first and greatest commandment. And the second is like it: 'Love your neighbor as yourself' " (Matthew 22:37-39). We simplify this principle for our little children as soon as they are aware of their fingers – "Jesus first, yourself last, and others in between."

Easily said, but not easily done. Our very human nature rebels against the order, especially for Americans. We are an arrogant lot (just ask foreigners). After all, we are citizens of the "land of the free and the home of the brave." We have those inalienable rights to "life, liberty and the pursuit of happiness." Free becomes "free to do what I want to do when I want to do it." So we throw our trash down for someone else to pick up; we speed down the interstate with our illegal anti-radar devices; and we call in sick to our bosses when we are not. Brave becomes "you kick sand in my face, I'll kick it back in yours." So we yell taunts at the umpire at our kid's softball game; we tailgate the little white-haired man who is holding up traffic; and we file a lawsuit if we think we have been unfairly treated. And, the pursuit of happiness is the real kicker! We must have a larger house, a more expensive car, a bigger boat and all the latest technology because we are not happy if someone else has more than we do. It is so easy to get on this merry-go-round, and so difficult to turn loose and step off. Our entire society is geared to getting ahead, pushing ourselves to the top of the corporate ladder, no matter whom we step on or who gets in our way. We must learn that true happiness can be found in one two-letter word that we have long forgotten: No!

Self-Sacrifice

What are you willing to give up for Christ? Your home? Your job? Your physical comforts? All your worldly possessions? Your friends? Your family? Your life? Christ tells us, "Anyone who loves his father or mother more than me is not worthy of me; anyone who loves his son or daughter more than me is not worthy of me; and anyone who does not take his cross and follow me is not worthy of me. Whoever finds his life will lose it, and whoever loses his life for my sake will find it" (Matthew 10:37-39). In other words, if we put anything before our Lord, we are not worthy of the sacrifice He made for us.

I am awed and humbled by sacrifices I see in fellow Christians. Consider, for example, a widow in Oklahoma who sold all her earthly possessions to move to Albania to work in the mission field. She had no promise of support for her work but went anyway, trusting in the Lord to take care of her. Her sacrifice belittles any sacrifice I have made, yet hers in no way compares with what Christ gave up for both of us. In much the same way that Ananias and Sapphira lied to Peter and to the Holy Spirit, we lie to ourselves. We take out our checkbooks and figure 10 percent of our net income, drop a check in the collection plate, and think that we have sacrificed for the Lord. God doesn't want our money; He wants our lives! It is true that giving is necessary and commanded to carry on the work of the church (we can even lend support to the widow from Oklahoma), but God wants us – all of us, inside and out, with all our baggage – to be used in His service for the benefit of others. For example, like Lydia in Philippi, our homes should be open to others at all times. I can find a dozen excuses, can't you? The house is a mess, I haven't dusted lately, I haven't been to the grocery, the dishes aren't washed, there's a good TV show on tonight, the kids have homework, I am too tired after working all day, and on, and on and on. We worry too much about appearances and our own selfish needs when we should have a continuous open-door policy. Our homes are not ours; they are God's.

Neither are our automobiles. An automobile should never be a status symbol. It should be an object that transports me (and others) and my belongings (and others') from point A to point B. I was blessed to have a wonderful Christian father who knew who really owned his car. As a child and a teenager, we attended, not the larger church within a half mile of our home, but a tiny congregation 22 miles away that could only be reached on 16 miles of rough gravel road. Our purpose: to pick up young preachers in training from David Lipscomb College who arrived from Nashville on a bus and then transport them to their pulpit.

When we started attending the country congregation, it had eight people in attendance. It grew to 60, and then as people moved away to more urban areas, it fed congregations elsewhere with dedicated Christians to work and worship. Many of those in attendance rode in my dad's car. I can remember being crammed with other children in the back seat – one Sunday 11 of us were transported to worship at one time! When Dad was asked if he worried about ruining his car with its load of passengers on such bad roads, his reply was, "God will give me another one when this one wears out." Not to leave my mother out, we often fed those same young preachers before putting them back on the afternoon bus.

How different we are today! How closed up in our own little worlds! We cannot serve others in isolation, yet we are more isolated today than ever before. We have moved the welcoming front-porch swing to the fenced-in backyard deck, and we rarely even use that! We have substituted the mechanical (church websites, e-mail, answering machines, phone trees) for the personal (the home visit, the small group Bible study, the Sunday dinner invitation). Everyone is too busy because we have failed to use the magic two-letter word *No*. Perhaps this is why the growth of the church has slowed in the last two decades – we are failing in our personal message to the world around us. We are failing to relate to other people, both in and out of the body of Christ, the glorious message of a sacrifice so magnificent that it has changed our lives to the point that "free" means "set free from sin" (Romans 6:18), "brave" means "I can do everything through [Christ] who gives me strength" (Philippians 4:13), and "pursuit of happiness" means "our citizenship is in heaven" (3:20). In other words, we have failed in our servitude.

How do we make a difference? Have you ever thrown a handful of pebbles in a lake and watched the circles get wider and wider until they touch each other and the ripples interlace? All of us within the circle of the church have our own circles of influence in the world. We must become up close and personal with all those within our circles until we have interlaced our earthly circles within the circle of the church. We must truly get to know people. We must open our homes and our hearts. We must make the effort to find areas of service, and then we must serve.

Philippians 2:9-11 tells us that because Christ so willingly submitted Himself to the will of His Father through His death on the cross, He was exalted in heaven to the highest place. God will also reward us if we have the same attitude as Christ. Our reward will be greater than anything we can imagine. All we have to do is submit and serve.

A CLEARER FOCUS

1. Explain in your own words the full nature of Christ's sacrifice.
2. Would the same temptations the devil used on Christ work on us? Why or why not?
3. How does the devil tempt us today?
4. Explain what it means to you personally to have the same attitude as Christ.
5. Is it more difficult for an American to have the same attitude as Christ than it is for a person in a Third World country? Why or why not?
6. Agree or disagree with the statement that we are more isolated today than in the past.
7. When was the last time you personally invited someone new to your home for the first time?

ABOVE AND BEYOND

- Look for an avenue of serving someone who is not a Christian. Serve that person this week.
- Invite someone to your home this week who has never visited you.
- Commit to memory Philippians 2:5-11.

LIKE STARS IN THE UNIVERSE

Philippians 2:12-30; 4:2-3

"Like stars in the universe, the lights innumerable
As symbols shine that we the true light win:
For every star and every deep they fill
Are stars and deeps within."
– George William Russell

On a recent trip to Wyoming, my husband and I drove for hundreds of miles along straight two-lane highways across rolling plains of sagebrush-dotted grasslands. Most of the time, except on open range, a fence paralleled either side of the pavement as a boundary to what seemed like endless acres of pasture for cattle. Despite the absence of a herd or even a stray cow or two, I noted one feature time and time again everywhere we drove. Just inside the pasture was a beaten path, worn dusty by the cattle as they traveled along the fence line. Why? Were they looking for a break in the wire so they could escape? Was the grass greener on the right-of-way? Why stay close to the fence when miles and miles of grass were available in the middle of the pasture? Perhaps it was the nature of the beast.

Perhaps for us, too, it is the nature of the beast. What is it in our human nature that makes us tread as closely to the fence and to danger as we possibly can? Rather than drawing to the center of our heavenly pasture where the Good Shepherd provides for our every need, we put ourselves in jeopardy by pacing the edge and gazing at the attractive dangers the world and Satan have to offer as if we are missing out on something. Perhaps we have not considered how serious this business of salvation really is.

Working Out Salvation

Paul says in Philippians 2:12 that we should "continue to work out [our] salvation with fear and trembling." Continue means we should persevere – "keep on keeping on." Salvation is an on-going struggle, not to be given up until we draw our last breath. Work is active. We cannot be lackadaisical or slothful in our pursuit of salvation. Salvation is not a passive acceptance of God's grace; it involves some action on our part with an attitude of fear and trembling. "Our God is an awesome God" (Wiegand 908) we sing with our youth, but lest we trivialize the power and majesty of God in the same way we have the word *awesome*, we must truly realize how weak and frail we are and how gracious He has been to us. Truly, we must tremble in His presence.

God told Isaiah that those who are esteemed in His eyes must be "humble and contrite in spirit, and tremble at my word" (66:2). Can you remember a time when you visibly trembled at the power of God's Word? I can. I was 10 years old. I knew I needed to step forward and accept Jesus as my Savior in baptism. A teenage girl several years older than I could see my distress from a pew at least 20 feet away. She silently mouthed, "Go ahead," and I did. Today, when I worship God, I may not visibly tremble, but my heart must tremble as I approach His throne with full recognition of who He is and who I am. And every day, I must live my life with a careful examination of where He stands and where I stand. Paul tells us in 1 Corinthians 10:12: "So, if you think you are standing firm, be careful that you don't fall." That means that when I think I am doing my best and standing closest to the Lord, I am in the most danger. Satan is always there, ready to trip me up. How many times have we been absolutely shocked by the fall of brothers and sisters in Christ who we thought would never leave their salvation behind? The truly shocking thing is it can happen to us, too! We must constantly be on guard lest we lose our souls. Christ Himself tells us, "No one who puts his hand to the plow and looks back is fit for service in the kingdom of God" (Luke 9:62). If disobedient angels were punished, "how shall we escape if we ignore such a great salvation?" (Hebrews 2:2-3). Working out my salvation is something only I can do. No one else can do it for me – not my preacher, not my husband, not my parents, not my friends. However, I am not alone in this working out. After I was crucified with Christ, "I no longer live, but Christ lives in me" (Galatians 2:20). Therefore, Paul says that "it is God who works in [me] to will and to act according to his good purpose" (Philippians 2:13). What a comfort! But, first, I must let Him work by making His will and my will one and the same.

Making His Will My Will

The only way we can will to do what God wants us to do is to know what His Will is. We must anchor ourselves in the Lord's Word through personal Bible study. Do you study God's Word? What is your purpose when you study? Is it to prepare to teach a children's class? A ladies class? Is it to answer the questions in a study guide? To write an article or a book? All of these reasons are well and good (and all certainly needed). Or is your study of the Bible to prove that "I'm right and you're wrong"? Heaven forbid! That attitude toward Bible study has closed more doors than we can ever open again. To be truly blessed, we must be like the righteous man in Psalm 1: "But his delight is in the law of the Lord, and on his law he meditates day and night" (v. 2). What makes this man truly righteous is his delight and meditation. In many cases, we have substituted a legalistic approach for a meditative one in our study of the Bible. Rather, we need to internalize its truths through quiet reflection and prayer. Try these suggestions.

(1) Choose a regular time for your study and meditation. Sometimes this is difficult, but with determination it can be done. Try getting up 30 minutes before everyone else or studying during your children's afternoon nap. What about lunch or break time at work? Find your time.

(2) Find your space. Christ went away from His disciples to lonely places to pray, and the man who prays in his closet is commended. Uninterrupted solitude is necessary but not always possible. (Do turn the cell phone off.) If your co-worker invades your private place to chat, firmly and sweetly suggest that you really need this time alone to survive the daily grind, or invite her to join you in prayer and Bible study (souls have been converted this way).

(3) Pray for guidance before and after reading the Word. Ask God to help you understand what He wants you to learn from your study, and then ask Him to help you put that knowledge into action.

(4) Make application of everything you read to your own life – not to others. Think: "God is talking to me personally in these scriptures."

(5) Plan the order of your study; then follow the plan. I have heard of those who simply flip open their Bibles and trust that their random choice is God's choice. Consider, for example, the young man whose Bible fell open to all the "begets" in Numbers and then asked his boss to let him off early from work to start his family immediately! A follow up of good works is usually admirable, but a little more structure to the plan of study would have certainly put those "begets" in context.

Changing our Bible study to a period of meditation on His Word will help us to "will and to act according to his good purpose" (Philippians 2:13). Only then will we shine "like stars in the universe as [we] hold out the word of life" (vv. 15-16).

Maximizing the Glow

How do we shine? We shine by not complaining about the trials the Lord places before us. Otherwise, we are like the Israelites who, after being saved from the bondage of Egypt, complained about every hardship on their journey to the Promised Land. These very adversities helped them to grow from weak slaves to strong warriors who could stand the heat of battle. Unlike them, we must accept without complaint the testing of our faith because it is that testing that strengthens us and "produces a harvest of righteousness and peace" (Hebrews 12:11). Through our example of acceptance and perseverance, we "stars" will also be smoothing the pathway for those following behind us "so that the lame may not be disabled, but rather healed" (v. 13).

We also shine by not arguing and debating among ourselves. Even in the Philippian church, this problem was occurring. In Philippians 4:2-3, Paul urges two women, Euodia and Syntyche, to get along with each other. It wasn't that they weren't good women or hard workers for the Lord – they simply disagreed with one another. Perhaps their personalities clashed. Paul certainly understood the situation because, at the beginning of his second missionary journey, he and Barnabas had disagreed sharply about John Mark. Their solution was to travel separately (Acts 15:39-40). Sometimes, a little distance is the only way to resolve differences of opinion, but it should always be done within the bounds of Christian love and without holding a grudge. Later, Paul commends Barnabas to the Corinthians for supporting himself as a preacher (1 Corinthians 9:6), and he asks Timothy to bring John Mark to him because of his faithful help in the ministry (2 Timothy 4:11). In the case of Euodia and Syntyche, Paul asks the other Philippians to help the women settle their differences so that the church can once again be viewed as harmonious in the eyes of the world.

Today we are also afflicted by argument and debate. Much of our time in group Bible study is often spent on matters that have no bearing on our salvation or the salvation of others. Some questions are left unanswered in the Bible, perhaps to make us study more diligently. Some are simply beyond our finite understanding. Some questions can be asked when we get to heaven (if we still think they are important, which we probably won't.)

At the same time, like the cattle in Wyoming, we need to stop testing the fence line. Through misplaced motives and a misunderstanding of our mission to bring the world to Christ, we want to move the fence, not the world. We debate the placement of the fence, and we argue about just how far out we can move it. We forget that it is safer to move toward the center – Christ – and leave the boundaries as God set them in His Word. Instead of bickering about what we can and can't do, our time would be better spent doing what we know we should do – holding out the word of life in its simplicity and purity as a beacon to bring the world in.

The only contact some people have with Christ is through watching Christians. The more we bicker among ourselves, the less attractive we are to the world. "Where is the peace that passes all understanding?" they wonder. By not complaining about our lot in life and by living at peace with one another, we will be seen as "blameless and pure, children of God without fault in a crooked and depraved generation" (Philippians 2:15). We will shine in the dark night of a sinful world in our feeble way, reflecting His glory.

Paul's Companion Stars

In the latter verses of Philippians 2 (vv. 19-30), Paul commends two "stars" who were working with him for the common cause of Christ during his imprisonment. Although we will look at Timothy's life more closely here, let us not overlook Epaphroditus who nearly died from his dedicated work for Christ.

Whether Epaphroditus exposed himself to an illness in his role as a servant or whether he simply worked so hard in his servitude that he weakened his immune system is not clear. In either case, he is cited by Paul as a role model of faithfulness to his Philippian church family. Epaphroditus stands as an example to us today. Although we are much more knowledgeable about how illnesses are spread in our society, we sometimes carry our caution too far. Definitely, we should never jeopardize the elderly or those already weakened by illness by visiting them when we are infected (perhaps a phone call will do) or by attending worship in close proximity to them. And, by all means, we should avoid shaking hands during cold and flu season (an apologetic smile works great and is less germ-ladened). However, we should not shirk our Christian duties by using our minor ailments as an excuse. In fact, if we make that little extra effort to get ourselves up and going, we will often be surprised at how much better we feel after experiencing the fellowship of our Christian family. We will also find that breathing deeply to sing praises to the Lord brings fresh oxygen to the physical body, a lift to the psyche, and healing to the soul. If we will make an effort, God will do the rest in making us feel whole again.

Paul writes at length about Timothy, calling him his son in Christ and praising him for looking not to his own interests but to Paul's needs and the needs of others. Timothy's devotion and dedication to Christ are due in part to the spiritual training he received from a good Jewish

grandmother and mother in his youth. Paul commends them indirect-
ly when he says to Timothy, "I have been reminded of your sincere
faith, which first lived in your grandmother Lois and in your mother
Eunice and, I am persuaded, now lives in you also" (2 Timothy 1:5).
Timothy was the son of a Greek father, obviously an unbeliever because Timothy was not circumcised as a child. Paul himself circumcised him as a young man, not from religious necessity, but to make
it easier for him to relate to the Jews he would be teaching about Christ.

Role Models for Today's Women

Lois and Eunice stand as models for all those mothers and grandmothers who "stand in the gap" alone when their husbands are either
absent, non-believers or unfaithful. Many women serve the Lord alone
today. I have watched many young mothers get themselves and their
children ready for Sunday school each week and then sit alone to cope
with their children through worship in the absence of a father. I have
often wondered how they do it, especially when the children are all
young, needing entertainment, wiggling and squirming, crying to leave.
What faith! What a responsibility! I think of all the help I had with our
two sons from their dad and am grateful that our children have two
Christian parents. May we never be critical of the single mom in church!

With or without Christian husbands and fathers, we mothers and
grandmothers can make such a difference in our children's lives, not
only by example but by teaching. If our children are "to will and to act
according to [God's] good purpose" (Philippians 2:13), it is up to us
to see that they have the tools necessary to use their Bibles for themselves. Too many of our children are non-readers. We must turn off the
television, the computer, and the video games and place a good book
in their hands. It takes effort to read, and many young people (especially boys) rebel at the idea, but we must insist.

Read aloud to your child, especially Bible stories, starting at a very
early age, and keep it up until your child is an independent reader. Then
switch roles: have your child read aloud to you from a Bible storybook
and other good literature. When selecting a Bible for your child, always accommodate her present reading ability: the International Children's Version of the Bible is at third-grade reading level, the New

International Version seventh-grade level, and the King James Version 12th-grade level. A child's vocabulary must be allowed to increase gradually; nothing is more discouraging than struggling with big words that a child cannot understand.

Make reading together a nightly activity, along with prayer, and you will be building a lifetime spiritual habit that will lead to independent meditation and study as an adult. I know a father who followed this plan when his daughters were little. Now, when he occasionally gets to check by their bedrooms at night (one is in college, the other a senior in high school), he often sees them with their Bibles in hand doing exactly what they were brought up to do. What a testimony to the perseverance and dedication he had in rearing his children in the Lord.

Only One Generation Away

We should all be like Epaphroditus and Timothy, and we should rear our children to be like them as well. The church is always one generation from apostasy. Consider, for example, how few Christians now live in the northeastern part of Kentucky where the Restoration Movement first took place. Somehow, in that area, the conflagration that swept across America lost its spark at the flashpoint. Rather than evangelizing the world, that area has to be evangelized. Praise is due those still living there who keep fanning the flame. If we lose the fire, we can lose the next generation of stars who must shine for Christ.

A CLEARER FOCUS

1. Why do we tread the fence today? What is the danger in this practice?

2. How do the world's religious practices affect our practice in worship and work? Name some traditions that we adhere to today that originated from other religious groups.

3. The two fastest growing religious groups today are the Mormons and the Muslims. Knowing the strict lifestyles of these two groups, what can we learn and apply to our own evangelistic efforts?

4. How do we go about making our "calling and election" sure (2 Peter 1:10)?

5. Explain in your own words exactly what working out salvation means.

6. Is it possible to know God's Word and not know God? What are some suggestions, other than those given here, for making our personal Bible study more meaningful?

7. Why is it important that our children develop good reading habits?

ABOVE AND BEYOND

- If you have not yet incorporated habitual daily prayer and meditation on God's Word into your daily routine, start immediately.
- Commit to memory Philippians 2:12-13.

8

HOVERING 'TWIXT NIGHT AND MORN

Philippians 3:1-11

"Between two worlds life hovers like a star,
'Twixt night and morn upon the horizon's verge."
– Lord Byron

Have you ever noticed how the same TV commercial is repeated over and over again? One I particularly noted advertised a medication to lower cholesterol. A slender, smiling lady, dressed in an evening gown, stepped out of a limousine and walked toward the camera while an orchestra played a memorable tune. Suddenly, she fell to the red carpet, I assume with a heart attack because of her high cholesterol. The full-length commercial played repeatedly for several weeks, then aired only on occasion. Instead, a shortened version showed her stepping from the limo while the melody played. We no longer needed to see her fall – we already knew the punch line.

In much the same way, Paul reiterates the main precepts he has already taught the Philippians. In fact, he says it is no trouble for him to repeat what he has told them before; after all, repetition of principles serves as a safeguard (Philippians 3:1).

We subscribe to this idea in theory and in practice. We repeatedly warn our children when they are young of dangers to their physical bodies (the hot stove, the busy street, the stranger's invitation). More importantly, as they grow older, we warn them about dangers to their spiritual bodies (addictions, sexual promiscuity, dating non-believers, false doctrines). The key, of course, in effective repetition is couching the message in different terms or in alternative modes, knowing that the learner has already been exposed to the basic principles being taught. Otherwise, the listener will tune us out.

Every preacher faces this problem in the pulpit. Most of his audience have already heard the truth, so he may choose a different mode of presentation to help them visualize that truth. Christ used a fig tree; today, we use Powerpoint. Or a preacher may simply approach his subject from a new or different angle. This is the approach Paul takes. Up to this point in his letter he has looked on the positive, spiritual side, commending the Philippians for their faithfulness and dedication to Christ. Now, he flips to the negative, worldly view that leads to discord, selfish ambition and legalistic righteousness.

Legalistic Righteousness

Paul begins by calling names – "dogs," that is. We have problems today seeing this as the ultimate derogatory term because of our beloved family pets; however, "dog" was the supreme insult to a Jew. The term has an interesting, and somewhat amusing, Old Testament history. As Goliath watched David approach him with his sling and five smooth stones, he asked, "Am I a dog, that you come at me with sticks?" (1 Samuel 17:43). Perhaps dog was not a low enough term for David because he later exaggerated the epithet in reference to himself when he asked King Saul, "Whom are you pursuing? A dead dog? A flea?" (24:14). In other words, if a dog is low, how much lower must be a flea on a dead dog. The Jewish Christians referred to by Paul in Philippians thought Gentile Christians were dogs because they ate any meat, whether clean or unclean, and were uncircumcised. Paul, however, turns the tables on these Jewish Christians by applying the term to them.

These Jews practiced what Paul terms "legalistic righteousness" (Philippians 3:6). They wanted to bind their ethnic and religious traditions on others, despite freedom bought by Christ's sacrifice. Their national and religious conceit came from centuries of tracing their lineage to Abraham and being called the "chosen" of God. Earthly pride in history and ritual had made their religious practices vain and empty. Paul understood them because, before knowing Christ, he had been one of them, placing all his trust in his Jewish résumé. He was "Hebrew of Hebrews" (v. 5). He took pride in his birth as a Jew (no proselyte here), in his proud lineage as a Jew (from the kingly tribe of Benjamin), and in his religious party (a Pharisee.) Add to that his zeal in applying the law, and he was the perfect judge and jury of his peers who strayed from the ancient teachings. In other words, he had built his reputation on the outward, worldly man and had put his "confidence in the flesh" (v. 4).

Don't we do this today? We arrogantly flaunt being an American in foreign countries, brag that we are from a particular region of the country, and act superior because of our political clout. We boast that we went to a specific university, have an advanced degree, or are members of a respected profession. We even research and write books tracing our lineage to the most famous foreigner we can find. Meanwhile, we add to our résumés a prestigious civic organization or two – the Lions Club, the Rotary Club, the Kiwanis Club, the Pilot Club – and assume as many offices and chairmanships as we possibly can. We work hard to be rewarded by the world with recognition, awards and promotions.

We don't stop with ourselves either. We ingrain this same set of worldly standards in our children. We want them to be the best and brightest at everything. We start early trying to get them in the most prestigious schools and tie up every minute of our time and theirs taking them to piano lessons, swimming lessons, gymnastics class, dance class and the ever-present sports teams. Some children grow up playing basketball, soccer, softball, tennis and golf and are given lessons from the time they are 6 years old in each. Meanwhile, we dress our primary school children in designer clothes, or whatever is the latest trend, so they will be in the "in crowd" at school. The trend continues through the teen years. We push them to build their résumés for a college scholarship by being a star athlete, a member of as many organizations as possible, and a top scholar all at the same time. If it all works out, we can brag about the university they got in and, later, about how much more money they make than we do. And then, we wonder why church attendance has dropped and our own children are leaving the Lord. Could it be because we and our children have put our confidence in the flesh? Could it be that we are guilty of legalistic righteousness? We take the heart out of the church when we place our hearts in the world. Worship becomes no more than a ritual performed out of duty, and the church becomes no more than a social club. We even list our church activities on our résumés to show what good people we are. Every politician wants to be affiliated with a church, and some even ask that a title be given them so they can use it in their political campaigns.

Seeking First Things First

Building a worldly résumé is not innately wrong as long as it does not take precedence over our spirituality. It is a matter of attitude and priority rather than activity. "Being proud" is different than "taking pride," which is the principle upon which we should base our lives and the lives of our children. Ultimately, the purpose behind everything we do must be to glorify Christ and His church. Why did I receive my education? So that I could use my abilities to reason out, study and communicate God's Word. Why did I become a public school teacher? So that I could be an example that Christ lives in me for my students, no matter the subject I teach.

Whatever our vocation in life, our first duty is not to gain worldly reward, but to demonstrate Christ living in us in all that we do. We must not strive to be the best doctor, lawyer, store clerk, secretary, receptionist or bank teller for worldly acclaim but to be known as a Christian doctor, a Christian lawyer, a Christian store clerk, a Christian secretary, a Christian receptionist or a Christian bank teller. Having the right attitude requires us to look up, not around or down.

Prioritizing Our Children's Lives

When we choose activities for our children, we must ask what the ultimate goal of that activity is: "How will it lead my children to serve Christ better as an adult?" If we ask that question, we may find ourselves prioritizing their activities differently than their worldly peer group. Certainly, every child should do her best in general education subjects with emphasis on developing reasoning, research and study skills that will enable her to delve into the depths of God's Word. Those same skills will serve her as well in her choice of vocation. A sport that develops teamwork skills and lifelong activity for a healthy body will enable her to work in unity within the church and maintain her physical body for the energy to serve others and Christ. Those same skills will serve her as well in her marriage and chosen vocation. Organizations and activities that develop leadership and speaking skills will help her to be able to teach and lead others to Christ. Those skills will also help her be able to supervise her children at home and/or peers on the job. Piano lessons will teach her to read music so that she can raise her voice in harmony with other Christians to praise God in song. Those skills will also give her lifelong enjoyment and entertainment. By placing our priorities in the right order, putting spiritual growth first, we will make choices for our children that will lead them to a life of service in Christ and success in the secular world as well.

By prioritizing, we will also be limiting the number of formal activities our children (and we) are engaged in by throwing out the dross (Psalm 119:119; Proverbs 25:4). We have so bought into the concept that our children will be behind that we have ignored common sense and the advice of psychologists and have overwhelmed our children with constant, organized activity. Children today have little or no free playtime, either in school or out of school. Where children once made up their own teams and rules for the game, we now dress them in uniforms with coaches and expect them to perform like pros. There is no time for imagination; there is no time for contemplation. How can our children ever understand the concept of "Be still, and know that I am God" (Psalm 46:10)?

More importantly, when does the family eat together, pray together and discuss the day's activities? Time spent driving our children to a ball park or a lesson, reading a book while waiting for them, or sitting in the stands watching them is not quality time spent with our children. We are merely chauffeurs and spectators. Strangely, the best day in our family was the summer our 10-year-old threw out his elbow pitching for Little League. Our older son had already given up organized sports because his awkwardness was derided by his teammates and unappreciated by his coach. The two boys began spending the summer together riding bikes, swimming in the creek, jumping on the trampoline in the backyard, and becoming the best of friends despite their 2½ year age difference. We had dinner together nearly every night with the entire family at the table at one time. This break from organized sports did not retard their physical development. In high school they both played tennis, and the younger became an all-district place kicker for the football team. Now in their early 30s, they are still best friends and enjoy golfing together. Some of their most cherished memories are of schedule-free summer days when they, and sometimes their friends from church and the neighborhood, played together in our backyard.

Prioritizing for ourselves and our children means getting off the merry-go-round and learning to say no to the world's standards and goals. Prioritizing means that we and our children understand "the whole duty of man" (Ecclesiastes 12:13). Prioritizing means time for spiritual things first and worldly things second – only inasmuch as they magnify the spiritual. Prioritizing means that everything we do calls attention to Christ and glorifies Him, rather than us.

Glorifying Christ in a Secular World

The American proliferation of secular good deeds makes it difficult to call attention to Christ and His church in today's world. It is hard to find a noticeable niche for the Lord while serving humanity. Our governmental programs (human services, public welfare) take care of the abused and poor; charitable organizations (often not associated with a religious group) provide clothing, soup kitchens and shelter for the homeless; assisted living homes and nursing homes take care of the infirm elderly; Meals-On-Wheels feeds the shut-ins; and civic organizations (Lions, Rotary, Kiwanis Clubs) fill in the gaps. Someone needs an expensive operation, and the community holds a car wash or a concert to help pay expenses. A flood washes homes away, and the Red Cross takes over. How can the Christian serve in these secular efforts (and we should) and at the same time give all the glory and honor to the true light – Christ – and His church?

The answer is simple, but it takes commitment. We must get up close and personal with people. Selling the Lord is a one-on-one campaign. Massive group efforts are impressive and often necessary to serve the physical and spiritual needs of the populace, but nothing works quite so well as the love and concern of one individual for another. In many cases, we try to hide ourselves in the anonymity of organizational efforts rather than taking it to the personal level where it counts the most. For example, when a tornado ripped through our small town, the church became a distribution point for the Churches of Christ Disaster Relief as well as for smaller contributions from other groups. "Two-pointers" in our fellowship gym became "pointing to" mattresses, stoves, refrigerators, food, clothing and toys for those who had lost everything. This made an impact on the community, and the church was seen as a caring congregation. However, the most vital impact was made by individual members or families who went to specific homes with rakes and shovels in hand to work alongside the victims in the cleanup effort. The personal bond of working together built relationships that ultimately had a greater impact for the Lord, opening doors for salvation. We must never forget that feeding the hungry, visiting the sick, helping the homeless, or aiding the elderly has an ultimate purpose: the saving of souls.

Throwing Out the Rubbish

Paul says that anything he lost to gain Christ was rubbish anyway (Philippians 3:8). The same is true for us. Our résumés are rubbish. They are merely lists on paper, actually leading nowhere. I have always been an obituary reader. Nothing underscores the brevity and tenuousness of life quite like reading obituaries. I scan each person's list of accomplishments, but I purposely look for one thing: Was he or she a Christian? The sobering fact is that few are. No matter how long our list of worldly accomplishments, they are nothing when placed alongside our salvation. Christ asks, "What good will it be for a man if he gains the whole world, yet forfeits his soul? Or what can a man give in exchange for his soul?" (Matthew 16:26).

Like Paul, we must no longer glory in our résumés, but rather in Christ's resurrection. We must take our prideful hearts out of the world and humble them at the foot of the cross. We must no longer dwell in an empty shell of religious ritual, but fill ourselves with His Spirit. Legalism and selfish ambition will give way to love if we prioritize our lives by seeking "first his kingdom and his righteousness" (Matthew 6:33).

A CLEARER FOCUS

1. Why is repetition important to our salvation? See Hebrews 10:24-27.

2. Jewish Christians demanding the tradition of circumcision for Gentiles was a divisive issue in the early church. Explain why Paul is so critical of the Jewish Christians in Philippians 3, yet he circumcised Timothy. See Acts 16:3; Galatians 2:3, 11-21.

3. Give some examples of traditions that some Christians are uncomfortable about changing. How do we know the difference in a tradition and a commanded practice?

4. If we have a problem solving a dispute over a tradition, what is the best way to handle the dispute?

5. What are practical suggestions for untangling ourselves and our children from overloaded schedules?

6. How can we work in secular organizations yet call attention to Christ rather than to ourselves or the organization?

ABOVE AND BEYOND

• Make a chart of your activities and/or your children's activities. Write down the spiritual goal for each one. Then prioritize your activities in order of spiritual importance.

• Much of the church is in turmoil today over practices that some call tradition and some call doctrine. You, more than likely, cannot explain why your congregation does or does not do something that other congregations of the Lord's church either practice or condemn. Take your Bible and research that practice. Read commentaries and, if possible, talk to or read the viewpoint of someone on either side of the debate. Settle the matter in your own mind and make sure that you can explain your position using the Scripture. Remember – if it is a tradition, you may change your mind later; if it is doctrine, you are not free to change.

9

FIXED TO A STAR

Philippians 3:12-16

"He who is fixed to a star does not change his mind."
– Leonardo da Vinci

I hate exercise. It seems such a waste of time. Jogging is certainly out of the question – I could never run without getting winded even as a child. I could choose to play a sport, but that requires an opponent or a team, and no one could possibly have enough patience to put up with my poor eye/hand coordination. Just ask my college badminton coach who offered me a C in physical education class if I would only keep class scores. The only exercise left for me is walking, but what an exercise in futility. Plodding in circles or on a treadmill like a hamster is walking to nowhere – there is no visible goal. Oh, I can tell myself about the physical benefits, but it is difficult to trick an inquiring mind that wants to know, "Where am I going?" That is why I am so glad that Christians have a goal.

For the Philippians with their Greco-Roman heritage, racing was probably the best analogy Paul could have used for the Christian life. The footrace was an important part of the Olympic games, which began approximately 800 years before Paul's writing. In fact, racing was the only event in the first 13 Olympiads. After that time, other games such as the discus and javelin throw, the long jump, wrestling, boxing and chariot racing were added, but the footrace was still regarded as the centerpiece of the Olympics. The prize in the ancient Greek games was a laurel wreath placed on the head of the winner. The games in Paul's day had been absorbed into Roman culture, and the prize included money as well. These games were finally halted in A.D. 394 because sports had become corrupted by violence and money. (Sound familiar?)

Despite the fact that footracing is outside the realm of the non-athlete's experience, it is an activity that anyone can understand. Certainly, the Philippians understood the principles of successful racing; it was a part of the sports culture of that day. Several passages in the New Testament letters use sports analogies, specifically boxing and racing, to teach about living the Christian life (i.e., 1 Corinthians 9:24-27; 1 Timothy 6:12; 2 Timothy 4:7-8; Hebrews 12:1-3). Paul's example of himself as a racer in Philippians 3:12-14, as well as other sports references, provides us with principles to guide us in the only true race for life.

Principle #1

• *We cannot be spectators; we have to enter the race.* I am amazed how fans at a football game automatically take credit for the victory: "Wow! Didn't we play a great game tonight?" Or "We put the hurt on them tonight, didn't we?" Or "We're number one!" The all-inclusive pronoun "we" does not include the spectators. We didn't do anything. We didn't run the ball or sack the quarterback or split the uprights. We watched from the sidelines.

We cannot watch from the sidelines if we want to get to heaven. We must first qualify for the race by putting on the proper attire, Christ. Paul says it best in his letter to the Romans: "[D]on't you know that all of us who were baptized into Christ Jesus were baptized into his death? We were therefore buried with him through baptism into death in order that, just as Christ was raised from the dead through the glory of the Father, we too may live a new life" (6:3-4). Baptism, putting on Christ, qualifies us to begin the race.

Once qualified to run, however, we cannot then choose to be a bench-warmer. Personal commitment is required. Without it, we can never claim the victory or the prize. We must fight "the good fight of the faith" and take "hold of the eternal life to which [we] were called" (1 Timothy 6:12). We must "continue to work out [our] salvation with fear and trembling" (Philippians 2:12).

Principle #2

• *We must keep in shape for the race.* Paul says in 1 Corinthians 9:25: "Everyone who competes in the games goes into strict training." Getting in shape and keeping in shape is not easy. It requires a proper regimen and diet.

A regimen is a strict plan for regulating diet and exercise to improve a person's health. We cannot properly train for the Christian race if we do not dedicate ourselves to a regimen based on Christ. We will not receive "the victor's crown" unless we compete "according to the rules" (2 Timothy 2:5). Nor can we run aimlessly or pretend we are exercising by "beating the air" (1 Corinthians 9:26). Following a regimen requires rules, discipline, focus and real effort. Paul says, "I beat my body and make it my slave so that after I have preached to others, I myself will not be disqualified for the prize" (v. 27). When we temper our earthly desires as Paul did, we are becoming godly, and "godliness has value for all things, holding promise for both the present life and the life to come" (1 Timothy 4:8). Meanwhile, we must also willingly submit to our heavenly Coach whose discipline will "strengthen [our] feeble arms and weak knees" (Hebrews 12:12). Ultimately, our spiritual body-building will enable us to run the course as Christ did because "everyone who is fully trained will be like his teacher" (Luke 6:40).

As part of our regimen, we must adhere to a healthy diet. First, like tiny babies, we need to "crave pure spiritual milk, so that by it [we] may grow up in [our] salvation" (1 Peter 2:2), but we cannot continue at this level without retarding our progress. To grow in strength, we must graduate from milk to solid food. The Hebrews writer says, "Anyone who lives on milk, being still an infant, is not acquainted with the teaching about righteousness. But solid food is for the mature, who by constant use have trained themselves to distinguish good from evil" (5:13-14). At the same time, we cannot fill ourselves with junk food and expect to have the spiritual strength we need to complete the race. Stamina comes from God's Word, not from a steady diet of soap operas, talk shows, magazines and paperback romances. A few sweets go a long way. Consuming the wrong food in large quantities will weigh us down with worldly thoughts and cravings, leaving no room for spiritual food.

Principle #3

• *Drop the baggage.* According to Hebrews 12:1, we need to "throw off everything that hinders and the sin that so easily entangles" us. Paul, using himself as an example of a Christian racer, tells us to forget "what is behind" (Philippians 3:13). In other words, we need to get rid of the baggage in our lives.

All of us carry baggage. To live in this world without messing up, or being messed up, once in a while is impossible. At some time, at some low point in our lives, we may even have committed a sin that we consider so vile that we simply can't believe God can forgive us, but He can and He will. We need only ask. And He expects us to believe that He forgave us. Were you abused as a child, physically or mentally? Forget it; it wasn't your fault. Were you involved in drugs or alcohol as a teen? Forget it. Were you involved in promiscuous behavior or did you have premarital sex? Forget it. Did you have a child out of wedlock or an abortion? Forget it. God has.

Why is it so difficult to give up guilt? More often than not, we find it easier to forgive others than to forgive ourselves. Accepting forgiveness is a part of faith. We must believe that Christ died for us, nailing humanity's sins – our sins – to the cross for all time. "Since we have now been justified by his blood" (Romans 5:9), we have "the forgiveness of sins, in accordance with the riches of God's grace" (Ephesians 1:7), and as long as "we walk in the light, as he is in the light, we have fellowship with one another, and the blood of Jesus, his Son, purifies us from all sin" (1 John 1:7). If God loved us enough to give His son to die for us so that He could forgive us, shouldn't we forgive ourselves? Drop the baggage.

Principle #4

• *Strain, push, reach for the next level.* Although Paul is referring to a spiritual straining to perfection, his analogy to a physical footrace certainly provides insight into the effort we must put forth. A friend of mine, Donna, has trained so that she can enter the local 5K races. At first, she spent hours alternating walking and running on a treadmill to build her stamina. Then, with a more experienced runner by her side, she was encouraged to set small goals along the way: just make it to the next block, or to that blue car parked beside the curb, or to the next intersection. She was amazed at the total number of miles she was able to run at one time, just by straining to reach each of these smaller goals.

We, too, must set spiritual goals for ourselves along the way. The Christian race takes daily effort, and each new day brings a new challenge for our spiritual growth. Sometimes the course has hills that we must struggle to climb. In Donna's first race, she almost became discouraged because she had practiced on level ground. How motivated she was when her trainer, who had already crossed the finish line, returned to her side to encourage her. Christ has already finished the race, too, and He runs by our side, offering the courage we need to keep on running. Sometimes heaven seems far away, appearing as a distant mirage on the hot, hard pavement of life. However, as we reach each new goal, we will draw closer to the reality of that final goal which will serve as an oasis for our souls.

Principle #5

• *Keep your eye on the prize.* I am ashamed to say how many times I have started through the house to change the clothes from the washer to the dryer and been sidetracked by other tasks. I see a dish that needs picking up in the den. I take it to the kitchen where I find more dishes to be put in the dishwasher. Then I see that the trash needs carried out, and while I am out-of-doors, I stop to pick up some limbs that blew off the tree the night before, and isn't the sunshine pretty today? I think I'll go get a cup of coffee and sit out here and read the paper. And, guess what? Two days later I find the mildewed clothes that must now be re-washed.

It is easy to be distracted by the little things in life, any of which may be truly important, and to forget where we are ultimately headed. This is especially true in running the Christian race. Like a horse pulling a carriage around Central Park in New York City, we need blinders for our peripheral vision to keep the bright lights and fast action surrounding us from diverting us from the course. We must stay focused. Nothing must come between us and our goal – not our family, not our friends, not our occupation, not ourselves. If we take our eyes off the prize, we will stray from the path. Thankfully, Christ's blood re-washes us as we get back on track, but such detours place us in danger of quitting the race altogether. Jesus said, "No one who puts his hand to the plow and looks back is fit for service in the kingdom of God" (Luke 9:62). We must be as single-minded as Paul who introduces the Christian race with the words, "But one thing I do" (Philippians 3:13).

Principle #6

• *The race isn't over until we reach the finish line.* The Christian race is a marathon. It isn't over until we are over – Jordan, that is, in the Promised Land. Amazingly, many people plan to retire to the bench (at the beach, in the mountains, etc.), pass the baton to the younger set, and sit out the rest of the race. Retiring isn't an option for the older Christian. Perhaps it is retirees to whom Jesus addresses His parable of the rich fool. We must not say, like him, in our later years, "[I] have plenty of good things laid up for many years. [I'll] Take life easy; eat, drink and be merry" (Luke 12:19). Our earthly work may be over, but our heavenly work is not. In fact, retirement is truly the golden years of work for the Lord. At last, we have plenty of time to visit the shut-ins, prepare and carry food to the sick and bereaved, make repairs on the house of worship, teach young women how to be good wives and mothers, mentor the children of the congregation, clean and stock the church pantry, grade correspondence courses, participate in Bible studies, and above all, encourage those who are less mature, both physically and spiritually, to continue toward the heavenly prize awaiting them.

Proverbs reminds us of what a blessing it is to reach physical and spiritual maturity in the Lord: "Gray hair is a crown of splendor; it is attained by a righteous life" (16:31). To that gray hair, then, when we have crossed the finish line, we can add "the crown of righteousness" given to us by "the Lord, the righteous Judge" (2 Timothy 4:8).

A CLEARER FOCUS

1. What does Paul mean by "I beat my body and make it my slave" (1 Corinthians 9:27)?

2. In 1 Peter 2:2 and in Hebrews 5:13-14, what constitutes milk and what constitutes meat in the Christian diet? Be specific. List several principles that might be considered milk and several that might be considered meat.

3. How does what we read and what we view affect our appetite?

4. What factors make it difficult for us to forgive ourselves?

5. What smaller goals might we set for ourselves along the way to help us grow spiritually?

6. Read the parable of the rich fool (Luke 12:16-21). How can this parable be applied to the modern-day retiree?

7. Read 1 Timothy 4:7-8. Explain how godliness holds promise for the present life.

ABOVE AND BEYOND

Evaluate yourself and your race for the prize:

- Where are you located on the Christian race track?
- What mile markers have you passed?
- Have you taken detours?
- If so, what got you back on track?
- Are you still attracted by those same temptations?
- More importantly, are you on track and focused on the prize now?

10

WANDERING STARS

Philippians 3:17-4:1

*"They are wild waves of the sea, foaming up their shame;
wandering stars, for whom blackest darkness
has been reserved forever" (Jude 13).*

I grew up in an age when most girls took four years of home economics in high school. We learned to cook and sew because we expected to marry, and cooking and sewing were, by the definition of that day, woman's work. In sewing class, we learned to pin a tissue pattern on the crosswise or lengthwise grain of a chosen fabric. Then we cut an identically shaped piece of cloth to be matched and sewn with other pieces into a skirt, blouse or dress exactly like the one pictured on the front of the pattern envelope. Certain markings on the pattern (i.e., darts, ease lines, notches) meant specific actions to be taken when assembling the parts of the garment. Not accurately marking these details or carelessly whacking with the scissors along the cut-line could mean wasted material or a dress that did not fit as intended. Therefore, to avoid having to wear a dress that looked home-made, I would apply the adage "measure twice, cut once" when I cut a garment by a pattern.

In Philippians 3:17, Paul urges the Christians at Philippi to follow not only his example but also the example of others "who live according to the pattern we gave you." Paul and those of whom he speaks were not doing their own thing. They were following a pattern. More specifically, Paul says, "Follow my example, as I follow the example of Christ" (1 Corinthians 11:1). The process of following a pattern encompasses the ideas of an original design by a creator, an unerring duplication process, and specificity in detail.

The Great Designer

God is the great Designer. We only have to look at the universe to admire the creative mind of God and to realize that our paltry attempts at art or composition can in no way rival His: "The heavens declare the glory of God; the skies proclaim the work of his hands. Day after day they pour forth speech; night after night they display knowledge" (Psalm 19:1-2). From the tiny stem cells that form the intricate parts of our bodies to the vast orbits of planets in faraway galaxies on the edge of Hubble's view, God has woven His designer's signature into the fabric of our physical universe. Just as cells divide a honeycomb, patterns exist within patterns, and like Ezekiel's "wheel intersecting a wheel" (Ezekiel 1:16), patterns emerge from patterns with the precision of a kaleidoscope governed by God's eternal laws.

The story of the Bible, recorded for more than 1,600 years by a multiplicity of authors, is filled with patterns within patterns, archetypes and types, symbols within symbols – all planned and designed before the world began. From the beginning, for example, Adam and Eve provided the pattern for the marriage relationship: "For this reason a man will leave his father and mother and be united to his wife, and they will become one flesh" (Genesis 2:24). In the New Testament, the marriage relationship that began with Adam and Eve and the church established by Christ co-exist as mutual patterns for each other:

> Wives, submit to your husbands as to the Lord. For the husband is the head of the wife as Christ is the head of the church, his body, of which he is the Savior. Now as the church submits to Christ, so also wives should submit to

their husbands in everything. Husbands, love your wives, just as Christ loved the church and gave himself up for her (Ephesians 5:22-25).

When Satan tempted Eve and sin entered the world, it was foreordained that God would send His Son to save mankind from that sin. The blood sacrifices of the Old Testament are an archetype for the ultimate blood sacrifice of Christ. His death, burial and resurrection in turn become a pattern for our baptismal death (Romans 6:3-7), bringing us in contact with that blood and marrying us to Christ. Patterns within patterns within patterns. It behooves us in particular to study the book of Hebrews, our CliffsNotes for the Old and New Testaments, which fully explains the relationship of God to humanity and His eternal, foreordained plan for us.

Duplicating the Designer Original

Clearly, God is a God of order, not chaos. He provides divine patterns for us to follow; and follow them we must in our spiritual growth; in our relationships with others; and in the organization, practice and mission of the church. Exact duplication, to the best of our ability, is necessary.

Although coloring outside the lines and thinking outside the box are encouraged in the secular world, those principles do not apply to following God's pattern. We must follow the cut-line where God has drawn it while measuring twice by carefully double-checking the instruction book. We cannot alter the pattern to fit our desires; we cannot update God's pattern because we think it is old-fashioned and we want to blend in with the religious world's latest trends. Rather we must redesign ourselves to fit His pattern. Otherwise, when we check our earthbound product against the heavenly example, we will find that ours is homemade and unrecognizable as a true, blood-bought designer original.

The Unidentified, Unspoken Sin

Ignoring God's plan and living outside the lines will make us "enemies of the cross of Christ" (Philippians 3:18), and our destiny will be destruction. Being a Christian means a pattern of self-denial, not excess. Paul puts it bluntly: "their god is their stomach, and their glory is in their shame" (v. 19).

Although Paul's reference to the belly or stomach can be more broadly applied to any sensual appetite – alcohol, prescription or other drugs, pornography, sex – that we might give precedence before service to God, it most definitely refers to overeating, a topic rarely addressed in the modern day pulpit. Many Christians are guilty of this sin – just take a look around while gathered in an assembly. Of course, we must admit that some people have a genetic predisposition to this problem, and there are other medical conditions that can lead to bloated figures. However, let us not be so quick to excuse ourselves. Our problem is more often one of self-indulgence. How can we possibly set a good example if we are overweight Christians trying to convert starving sinners? How can we show the world that we are disciplined people if we don't exercise and eat healthily? If we overindulge at the table or continue to make poor choices in our diet, although we know better, we are sinning!

Obesity is an epidemic of global proportions in all but Third World countries, affecting approximately 300 million people. In America the percentage of overweight people 20 years old and up did not change significantly between 1960 and 1980. However, between 1980 and 2000, the percentage increased dramatically. Empowered by the women's liberation movement, women began joining the work force in record numbers, prompting the growth of fast-food restaurant chains. Meanwhile, the push-button conveniences in the household, as well as other technological advances in manufacturing and agriculture, reduced the amount of physical labor necessary to complete a task, thus eliminating exercise. In addition, the me-generation attitude of selfish indulgence added stress, often dealt with through comfort food.

As a result, a 1999-2000 survey estimated that 65 percent of the American population over 20 are now overweight. More alarming is the significant growth of obesity in our children and adolescents that has tripled in the last two decades. The future is not bright when we consider the results of this trend. According to a Brown University study, 70 percent of overweight adolescents will become overweight or obese adults, which will translate into more heart disease, strokes and diabetes in adult years ("What You"). As Christian parents, we must limit the fried foods that are a staple of fast-food restaurants and the sugary cereals and snacks that are available in our homes. We must teach our children that their bodies are "a temple of the Holy Spirit" (1 Corinthians 6:19) and that certain foods are just as addictive as drugs and alcohol. In other words, as stated in a recent grocery store brochure, "Your body is your temple. And jelly doughnuts for breakfast are no way to worship [in] it."

Over-indulgence is nothing new. Xerxes staged a seven-day banquet for his nobles where he demanded Vashti to display herself before them (Esther 1:1-12). And Eglon, king of Moab, certainly had overeaten when Ehud's sword went into his belly so far that the fat closed over the handle (Judges 3:15-22). Until recent years, overeating and being overweight were only for royalty and the idle rich. In Elizabethan England, nobles actually padded their clothing over their stomachs to appear fatter and more prosperous. Today in America, overeating is associated with lack of discipline rather than with money. We are the nation of all-you-can-eat food bars where we stuff ourselves to be sure we get our money's worth. American Christians need to be like Daniel and his companions who certainly demonstrated godly restraint in turning down the rich, unclean foods provided by Nebuchadnezzar in Babylon (Daniel 1:5-16). Notice, they ate vegetables, the food group we ignore most today.

The results of our undisciplined eating habits are costly, both physically and spiritually. As Christians we can try to ignore that we are following this worldly trend. We can make jokes about our "see-food" diet and about living to eat instead of eating to live while we overload our plates at fellowship meals, but in doing so, we are part of the epidemic that is spreading to our children by our example. Proverbs 23:20-21 tells us not to join those "who drink too much wine or gorge themselves on meat, for drunkards and gluttons become poor, and drowsiness clothes them in rags."

More important than these physical results are the spiritual ones. Paul has identified Christians who practice gluttony as "enemies of the cross of Christ" who are doomed to destruction (Philippians 3:18-19). That is a serious condemnation.

Idols of Shame

Other qualities of Christians who are "enemies of the cross of Christ" are those whose "glory is in their shame" and whose minds are "on earthly things" (Philippians 3:19). We and our children, especially our teens, are bombarded on every side by digital idols who glory in their shame. I feel sorry for today's Christian parents who must bring up children "in the training and instruction of the Lord" (Ephesians 6:4). The television and the computer have invaded our safe little worlds where we were once able to protect our children from knowing too much too soon. How hard it is now to make choices, and how vigilant a parent must be.

In the 1980s, it was easier for Christian parents to rear children, although it was not easy even then. I remember when a lightning bolt hit the dish at our house and took out the receiver and all connections. Six hundred channels, including MTV, fried. Our sons, just on the edge of puberty, were limited from that day through their high school years to four local channels received by antenna. We used the dish as a giant birdbath. With the limited viewing, we could actually let our children have their own televisions in their bedrooms.

Not so today. Now even local channels are not safe. Among the worst offenders are sitcoms with their double-entendres (yes, the kids do get it!) and their promotion of premarital sex, drinking, homosexuality, drugs and promiscuous dress. Meanwhile, talk shows glorify conflict and violence, and reality shows enhance those qualities through gossip and underhanded maneuvering to do whatever is necessary to win. Even the news has taken on a tabloid flavor, carrying stories of perversion with graphic pictures that young children should not see. We want our young people to have a grasp of world geography, political systems, business and governmental issues so that they can become informed citizens, yet they learn instead about murder and mayhem, insider trading deals, oral sex with interns, and lying through semantic wordplay. No wonder the younger generations are so cynical.

Christian mothers and fathers must also prevent their children from glorying "in their shame" (Philippians 3:19) by holding the line at each new fashion trend despite the fact that their daughters wail about being ostracized because they can't dress in the latest fads. Some fashions are harmless and will, thankfully, disappear with time, but many give a come-on message to young men with raging hormones and older men who may prey on young girls. Pop singers should be no girl's role model – just ask any teacher or school administrator who deals with permissive mothers while enforcing a dress code. Trendy teen girls' fashions are always either too short, too low or don't meet in the middle. Certainly, a Christian mother should never be caught defending her child's clothing against a school dress code.

Boys are not exempt. Underwear is what it is called: under wear. And, as a parent, if we are not up on the latest sexual slang terms, we need to get that way fast before shopping for T-shirts with messages. Many times, young men don't realize that adults have been around the block once or twice and do understand the message on a shirt. Certainly, a Christian young man should not offend anyone by wearing messages or images that even hint at violence, racial or gender bias, or sexual harassment.

Paul describes much of today's society when he tells Timothy that in the last days people will be "lovers of themselves, lovers of money, boastful, proud, abusive, disobedient to their parents, ungrateful, unholy, without love, unforgiving, slanderous, without self-control, brutal, not lovers of the good, treacherous, rash, conceited, lovers of pleasure rather than lovers of God – having a form of godliness but denying its power" (2 Timothy 3:1-5).

We should take no part in these types of behavior, nor should we voice our admiration for those who do these things. Unfortunately, the world calls them celebrities.

Our duty is to keep our minds and the minds of our children focused on heavenly, rather than earthly, things. Why? Paul says, "Our citizenship is in heaven" (Philippians 3:20).

There Christ will "transform our lowly bodies so that they will be like his glorious body" (Philippians 3:21). If we are numbered among those "who wash their robes," we "may go through the gates into the city" (Revelation 22:14). Therefore, we must "stand firm in the Lord" (Philippians 4:1) and "live according to the pattern" (3:17).

A CLEARER FOCUS

1. Make a list of patterns, archetypes and types, or symbols in the Bible. Use the book of Hebrews to stimulate your thinking.

2. God is a God of order, not chaos. What are some ways that we introduce chaos ...

   a. into our personal lives?

   b. into our relationships?

   c. into the church?

3. Is it more difficult to control bad eating habits than it is to control other addictions? Why or why not?

4. What are some practical suggestions for controlling bad eating habits for us and our children?

5. What are some practical suggestions for TV viewing and Internet use for ourselves and our children?

6. What are some practical suggestions for dealing with our children and fashion trends?

7. How can we minimize the effect of celebrities (i.e., rock stars, actors) on our children?

ABOVE AND BEYOND

• Check the latest weight charts and weigh yourself against them. You may be surprised to find that you are considered overweight or obese. If so, begin an exercise regimen and watch your diet.

• Check the nutritional information on the foods in your kitchen cabinets. Eliminate those foods that are unhealthy for you and your children. Each time you grocery shop, check labels before making purchases. Even people in the healthy weight range may have fat arteries. Keep a check on your cholesterol levels.

• Ask restaurants to provide you with a calorie count for specific items on their menu. Although they may not have the information available (which they should), you have made them aware of your concern about the ingredients they use.

11

PEACE DIVINE LIKE QUIET NIGHT

Philippians 4:4-7

"Joy is like restless day; but peace divine Like quiet night; Lead me, O Lord, – till perfect Day shall shine, Through Peace to light."
– Adelaide Anne Procter

Horatio G. Spafford experienced more heartache in his lifetime than most of us can even imagine. After the death of his son and the loss of his real estate in the great Chicago Fire of 1871, he decided that he, his wife and four daughters should take a European vacation. Last minute business prevented him from traveling with them on the *S.S. Ville du Havre*, so he sent them ahead and rebooked his voyage on a different ship. A few days after his family sailed, he received a cable from his wife stating simply, "Saved alone." Their ocean liner had been struck by another ship and had sunk in 12 minutes. His four daughters were dead. Out of this painful experience came the lyrics of one of the most powerful hymns we sing:

When peace like a river, attendeth my way,

When sorrows like sea-billows roll,

Whatever my lot, Thou hast taught me to say,
"It is well, it is well with my soul" (Osbeck 127).

Paul says, "[T]he peace of God, which transcends all understanding, will guard your hearts and your minds in Christ Jesus" (Philippians 4:7). This peace is so powerful that we cannot fully understand it. However, if we have the peace of God in our lives, as well as other attributes that attend it, the world will want what we have. The qualities that Paul describes in Philippians 4:4-7, when displayed by a Christian, will convert more souls than all the preaching from our pulpits.

Praying Our Way to Peace

How do we attain this perfect peace of God? Paul says that it depends on our prayer life. We are to pray about everything, presenting our petitions to God with thanksgiving. "Be joyful always; pray continually; give thanks in all circumstances" (1 Thessalonians 5:16-18). James says, "Come near to God and he will come near to you" (4:8). As a result of this intense prayer life, we will be guarded by a perfect peace, having more spiritual benefits than our finite minds can understand.

We have only to look at Christ, our perfect example, to understand how important prayer is. Christ communed with His Father regularly in private, intense prayer. His normal practice was to withdraw to a lonely place (Luke 5:16), often on a mountainside (6:12; 9:28; 22:39), and pray for long periods of time, sometimes all night (6:12). He prayed when He was full of joy (10:21), and when He was anguished (22:44). Even His physical body attitude, kneeling or prostrate on the ground, demonstrated His subjection to His heavenly Father (v. 41; Matthew 26:39). The oneness of Christ with God gave Him the perfect peace necessary to stand mute before His accusers and to suffer death without a murmur. Earlier in His ministry, the disciples had observed the strength He drew from prayer and asked Him to teach them to pray (Luke 11:1). The more complete version of that model prayer is found in Matthew 6:9-13:

• *"Our Father in heaven, hallowed be your name."* We must recognize who God is, reverence His name, and truly understand what He means when He says, "As the heavens are higher than the earth, so are my ways higher than your ways and my thoughts than your thoughts"

(Isaiah 55:9). We must, at all times, acknowledge how great and powerful God is, as Daniel says, "I prayed to the Lord my God and confessed: 'O Lord, the great and awesome God, who keeps his covenant of love with all who love him and obey his commands' " (Daniel 9:4).

• *"[Y]our kingdom come."* We must believe that God sent His Son to establish His kingdom on earth – the church, which is as close to heaven on earth as we can get. Being in that kingdom means sharing "in the inheritance of the saints in the kingdom of light. For he has rescued us from the dominion of darkness and brought us into the kingdom of the Son he loves, in whom we have redemption, the forgiveness of sins" (Colossians 1:12-14).

• *"[Y]our will be done on earth as it is in heaven."* "Your will be done" is not an empty phrase but a lifestyle. If we are to have the same inner peace that Christ had, we must first submit our will to His will as we pray. John says, "[I]f our hearts do not condemn us, we have confidence before God and receive from him anything we ask, because we obey his commands and do what pleases him. And this is his command: to believe in the name of his Son, Jesus Christ, and to love one another as he commanded us" (1 John 3:21-23).

• *"Give us today our daily bread."* We must take everything to the Lord in prayer. Sometimes we have the attitude that our daily concerns are too petty for us to bother God. However, every problem, no matter how small, should be turned over to Him. Only by giving our cares to Him will we know true peace. We are to petition God for our needs, knowing that He will give us what is best (Matthew 7:9-11). This is not to say that we present Him with a grocery list of selfish desires but that we ask Him to work His will in us as is most needful and best for our spiritual growth.

• *"Forgive us our debts, as we also have forgiven our debtors."* Forgiveness of others means submission to God. "For if you forgive men when they sin against you, your heavenly Father will also forgive you. But if you do not forgive men their sins, your Father will not forgive your sins" (Matthew 6:14-15). We cannot hold grudges. We cannot take revenge, nor can we wish for others to take revenge for us. We cannot even ask God to avenge the wrongs of others; that is His business: "It is mine to avenge; I will repay" (Hebrews 10:30). However, we can give our injured hearts over to God, and He will heal us.

• *"And lead us not into temptation, but deliver us from the evil one."* Paul tells us, "God is faithful; he will not let you be tempted beyond what you can bear. But when you are tempted, he will also provide a way out so that you can stand up under it" (1 Corinthians 10:13). How much more powerful is this promise when we are filled with the perfect peace of God because it will guard our hearts from further temptation.

Meanwhile, all our requests to God should be made with thanksgiving (Philippians 4:6), trusting Him to give us the best answer whether it is "yes" or "no" or "not at this time." Paul says in 1 Thessalonians 5:18 to "give thanks in all circumstances, for this is God's will for you in Christ Jesus." Even when we are suffering hardship or sorrow, it should be with a thankful heart that we pray, knowing that "all things work together for good to them that love God, to them who are the called according to his purpose" (Romans 8:28 KJV). A thankful heart recognizes God's presence working in our best interests which in turn produces the inner peace that is beyond our understanding.

The Living Water Within

When the peace of God reigns in our lives and guards our hearts, three beautiful qualities pour forth from the well-spring of the quiet living water within us: we accept the turbulence of life without anxiety, we gently provide calm for those around us, and our joy in the Lord overflows in abundance (Philippians 4:4-6).

Worry and anxiety are temporal traits, and the world knows them well. Truly, we all have problems and stress. However, it has been said that half the things we worry about never happen and the other half are beyond our control anyway, so why worry? Women, it seems, are more prone to anxiety. Men are better able to compartmentalize their lives, not letting one area spill over into another. We are different. We take problems from home to work and from work to home, our minds filled with too many "if onlys" and "I wish I hads." Even harder, perhaps, is to put aside our worry about sudden, unexpected events. We tend to think the worst before we have all the facts. In my own experience, I cannot count the times that I thought my children were in an accident just because I heard a siren or they were late coming in. One time I an-

swered my door, white-faced and trembling, for a highway patrol-
man who had come to the wrong house.

A spirit calmed by the peace of God does not expect the worst, but
rather the best, because we know that God is good and that we can cast
all our anxiety on Him because He cares for us (1 Peter 5:7). Christ
Himself asked, "Who of you by worrying can add a single hour to
his life?" (Matthew 6:27). It is true that one of my children could have
been killed in an automobile accident, but I could have done nothing
to prevent it. Our comfort in the Lord at such devastating times of loss
is knowing that there is a plan – a pattern – much larger than ourselves
that we cannot see because we are a part of it and that the Planner who
views the total design will give us the comfort of His love and peace
to assuage our grief.

That same peace of God will display itself in our gentle and quiet
nature. To gentle a horse is to put its power under control. We, too, have
the power to hurt others; however, we have been gentled by a loving
Savior. Therefore, we will not participate in office gossip or spread
tales or rumors, whether true or untrue. We will not be sarcastic or rude.
We will give the gentle answer that turns away wrath. We will listen
quietly and respectfully to opposing viewpoints without interrupting.
We will not raise our voice to be heard over others. We will use the
magic words – "please," "excuse me" and "thank you" – often. We will
be patient while standing in a long check-out line. We will let others
who have only one or two items ahead of us. We will not cut someone off to get a parking space. We will not tailgate or angrily honk when
other drivers make a mistake. We will generously tip the waitress despite the slow service in the kitchen. We will not argue with the po-
liceman about a ticket. We will not suspect all lawyers and politicians
of greed and shady dealings. We will give everyone the benefit of the
doubt. Being gentle is not easy, especially if our lives lack Christian
joy or if we are worried or anxious. The gentleness of Christ is our goal.

Evidence of Joy

"Rejoice in the Lord always. I will say it again: Rejoice!" (Philippians
4:4). We will truly rejoice if we have the peace of God. Philippians is
known as the book of joy; 16 times rejoicing is mentioned in various

forms. Joy is not mere happiness that comes as a result of external events; rather it comes from within. Happiness is temporary, but joy is lasting. Therefore, if we rejoice in the Lord, it will always be evident to the world around us. In worship, we will not bury our heads in the hymnal with a down-in-the-mouth, somber attitude. Instead we will sing praises to God and His Son Jesus with our spirits lifted heavenward and no gloom and doom dark cloud hanging over our heads. "O How I Love Jesus" will bring a sparkle to our eyes. Our joy will be evidenced by our cheerful hearts and quick smiles.

Even in adversity we can find joy. Think of Paul and Silas beaten and in jail in Philippi, rejoicing in song (Acts 16). James says, "Consider it pure joy, my brothers, whenever you face trials of many kinds, because you know that the testing of your faith develops perseverance" (1:2). Although we may be saddened by the occurrence of some event, we will find joy through our comparison to what could have been and in our anticipation of what will be. For example, when our house burned in 1979 with very little saved, we rejoiced that our two sons, who could have been tempted to return to the burning house to save their Christmas toys, and my invalid father had made it out safely. One month later while scouting for new appliances, my husband and I saw a child with no legs and thanked God for blessing us with two healthy children. Through our experiences we have been able to share tips with others (i.e., store photo negatives in another location) and have been able to help those who have more recently lost their homes. Joy is there, even in tragedy, if we only tap its source.

The more we commune with God and increase in faith and knowledge, the more joy, gentleness and peace will grow. These traits are opposite to what our human nature would have us be. However, through an active, intense prayer life, based on Christ's teaching and example, we will tap into the peace of God. That peace will guard our minds from the influences of evil and will make us shine like stars in the universe for all to see. Truly, we will be able to say, "It is well, it is well with my soul."

A CLEARER FOCUS

1. Explain the difference in happiness and joy.

2. Give personal examples of people with whom you associate joy. Or gentleness. Or peace.

3. What hinders joyful living?

4. What situations test our gentle, forbearing spirit? What are practical suggestions for avoiding the negative effects of these situations?

5. Why is gentleness one of the qualifications of an elder?

6. What are some short-term and long-term effects of anxiety?

ABOVE AND BEYOND

• Examine your life. Do people think of you as joyful? As gentle? As peaceful? What do you need to do to internalize these qualities so that they will shine in your life?

• Commit to memory Philippians 4:4-7.

SHIMMERING STARS, SHINING SOULS

Philippians 4:8-9

"In the profound unknown, Illumined, fair, and lone,
Each star is set to shimmer in its place.
In the profound divine Each soul is set to shine,
And its unique appointed orbit trace."
– Bliss Carman (1861-1929)

As a young bride in a new home, my first flower garden was to feature phlox. I had never grown phlox, but I could tell by the picture on the Ferry Morse seed packet that they would be beautiful along the foundation of our front porch. My husband worked up the soil, and I carefully planted a row of seeds. When the little plants appeared, I thinned them and transplanted a few to make an even row extending the full length of the porch. As the plants grew, I compared their leaves to the packet picture. Something was wrong. The plants were different. They continued growing until one day my husband observed, "Sure does look like poke salad to me!" He was right. I will never know how seeds for a common southern weed ended up in a Ferry Morse seed packet, but they did, and I had a wonderful, well-cultivated row of pokeweed reaching to the roof and shading our front porch. (We let it grow because the whole incident was so funny.) It was a perfect example of Galatians 6:7: "A man reaps what he sows."

The same is true for what a person plants in the heart. Proverbs 4:23 says to "guard your heart, for it is the wellspring of life." In other words, what you put in your heart will ultimately determine what will come out of your heart. The adage that comes to mind is a negative one: "Garbage in, garbage out." You are what you think. Paul tells us in Philippians 4:8 to keep our minds focused on those things that are true, noble, right, pure, lovely and admirable. Along with an intense prayer life, thinking about these virtues will help to prepare our minds and hearts for the peace of God mentioned in verse 7.

But what do true, noble, right, pure, lovely and admirable mean? Such qualities are sometimes difficult to define because they are intangible. However, like the wind rustling the leaves, we may not see the force itself, but we recognize the effects. We may not know exactly what it is, but we do know it when we see it in action. Proverbs 23:7 says that as a man "thinketh in his heart, so is he" (KJV). We may test what is in our hearts by looking at our actions, for they will tell the tale.

Whatever Is True

Truth is defined as "that which is reliable, trustworthy, and consistent with the character and revelation of God" (*Nelson's*). By design, Paul lists truth as the first and ultimate quality. All others are based on this one quality that is anchored in God's Holy Word. Today's world has duped us into believing that there is no such thing as absolute truth. Kenneth L. Woodward, in a *Newsweek* article titled "What Is Virtue?", says that "we live in an age of moral relativism. ... [We have] reduced all ideas of right and wrong to matters of personal taste, emotional preference or cultural choice. Since the truth cannot be known, neither can the good" (38). Jean Bethke Elshtain, a professor of political science at Vanderbilt University, says, "You can't have strong virtues without strong institutions. And you can't have strong institutions without moral authority" (Woodward 39).

As members of Christ's body, we must not buy into the philosophy of moral relativism that pervades the religious world around us where no one is excluded or offended and anything goes. Consider, for example, how insidious the growth of such a philosophy is by examining recent practices in some major denominations.

First, being pressured by the National Organization of Women, these groups opined that the Bible does not mean what it says about women's roles in the church (1 Corinthians 14:34), and now women serve as ministers in their pulpits and in other leadership roles. As a further step, because the Bible does not mean what it says anyway, some of these same groups have acquiesced to homosexual rights supporters and have allowed homosexuals in their pulpits and in leadership roles as well (Romans 1:24-27).

Although the Lord's church has not fallen so far from biblical teaching, we continuously flirt with danger by allowing this same disdain for moral authority and absolute truth to invade the body. We have members who treat the church and its leadership as if it were a worldly institution. They question whether the Bible means what it says about even the most basic principles. They deny the authority of the eldership as shepherds overseeing the local church. They view the Lord's church as just another denomination. What a burden we place on our bishops when we allow worldly attitudes to influence our spiritual practices. How much more vigilant they must be to "hold firmly to the trustworthy message as it has been taught" so they can "encourage others by sound doctrine and refute those who oppose it" (Titus 1:9).

To think on things that are true, we must go to the source of truth – the infallible Word of God. We must not be taken in by the beautiful pictures and false labels with which the religious world packages its lies. We must "hold firmly to the faith we profess" (Hebrews 4:14) and follow the pattern for our lives and the church as it is set forth in the holy pages of God's Book.

Whatever Is Noble

Noble is also translated *honest* (KJV); *honorable* (NASB); *worthy of reverence ... seemly* (AMPLIFIED). The aristocracy of various countries has long been called the nobility but has not necessarily embodied the character that the word implies. Brian R. Price translates the quality of nobility from the medieval "Code of Chivalry for Knighthood" as "seek[ing] great stature of character by holding to the virtues and duties of a knight, realizing that though the ideals cannot be reached, the quality of striving towards them ennobles the spirit, growing the character from dust towards the heavens. Nobility also has the tendency to influence others, offering a compelling example of what can be done in the service of rightness."

Being noble, in other words, means knowing the right thing to do, then doing it. Therefore, nobility of character implies honesty, dignity and decorum in behavior which ultimately leads to respect, honor and veneration even from a worldly point of view. Honesty is basic: our word must be our bond; there should be no necessity for contracts or other legal documents. Unfortunately, a word and handshake are no longer considered binding by today's standards. Not so for a Christian: "Simply let your 'Yes' be 'Yes,' and your 'No,' 'No' " (Matthew 5:37), which makes the legalities required by law superfluous.

At the same time, a Christian should always behave with dignity and decorum. This is not to say that we are humorless or stiff in our dealings with others. Rather, we are to be warm and approachable. Meanwhile, we will not engage in coarse or vulgar humor nor in gross behavior that even the world finds disgusting. As Paul tells the Ephesians, "But among you there must not be even a hint of sexual immorality, or of any kind of impurity, or of greed, because these are improper for God's holy people. Nor should there be obscenity, foolish talk or coarse joking, which are out of place" (5:3-4). Furthermore, the Christian will recognize the level of formality deemed suitable for various situations and choose appropriate language and manners to suit the circumstances. One does not talk about one's incontinence problems at a wedding tea although such a problem might be shared privately with a friend at home. Meanwhile, some things are simply not shared ever outside the home!

Whatever Is Right

Right, also translated as *just* (KJV, AMPLIFIED) is defined as "that which is just and fair" or "correct." It finds its basis in the word "righteous," which means "without guilt before God [or] acting according to God's laws" (*Nelson's*). Therefore, right is about obeying the laws of God and of government. We must always ask, "What is the right thing to do?"

Right is absolute, unmodified by circumstance; it is not relative to the situation. Right is right. Right will not allow us to defraud an insurance company. Right will not allow us to be paid in cash to hide income from the Internal Revenue Service. Right will not allow us to pull strings to get our child an unfair advantage over others because we know the right people. Right will not allow us to take sick leave when we want a day off. Right will not let us download files illegally from the Internet. Right will not let us "scratch their back if they scratch ours" in underhanded business deals or politics. Right will not let us make pirated copies of tapes, CDs and DVDs. Right will not let us plagiarize the words or ideas of others without giving credit to the source. Right will not let us get a speeding ticket fixed.

Being just and fair will also prevent us from stereotyping others based on income, background, ethnicity or appearance. We will accept each individual on the evidence of her own worth in the sight of the Lord. Often we are blinded by our own prejudices, but the justice and fairness of Christ's example should guide us in our treatment of others.

Whatever Is Pure

Whenever we sing the hymn, "Purer in Heart, O God," I am always struck by a phrase in Fannie E.C. Davison's lyrics: "Keep me from secret sin" (Wiegand 542). It reminds me that I can sin with no one (but God) knowing about it. The word *pure* means "uncontaminated; not containing any mixture of evil; unmixed" (*Nelson's*). We use the word mostly in relation to water. We are concerned about our drinking water containing even trace elements of contaminants that might harm our bodies. For that reason, many of us drink filtered water.

If we are so concerned about the purity of the water we drink, we certainly should be concerned about the purity of our thoughts. If we feed them with contaminants, our thoughts will become poisoned. Reading books or viewing films that appeal to our sexual appetites can make our thoughts so impure that we replace our flesh and blood husbands with fantasy men – or worse, real men. Sex therapists such as Dr. Ruth suggest that it is okay for married women to fantasize about a handsome male star while having sexual relations with their husbands. Sounds like adultery to me (Matthew 5:27-28). We need to filter our thoughts through the cleansing power of prayer and avoid those materials which appeal to our base instincts.

Whatever Is Lovely

Lovely is also translated "and loveable" (AMPLIFIED). "Aren't the flowers lovely?" "What a lovely sunset." "You have a lovely smile." "What a lovely dress." "Isn't that a lovely painting?" "Lovely" is a difficult word to define, but we know "lovely" when we see it. A dictionary definition includes "having pleasing or attractive qualities; beautiful; graceful," and "enjoyable; delightful" (*American Heritage Dictionary*). Although the definition includes the word *beautiful*, something can be beautiful, but not lovely. For example, a coral snake is beautiful, but it certainly isn't lovely because it inspires fear. Lovely, therefore, must evoke our admiration through color and design while, at the same time, inspiring our emotions and elevating our spirits through an appeal to our higher instincts. Within our psyches, God has internalized a recognition of design, balance and symmetry in the arts and in nature that elicits a deep, emotional response that strips the veneer of daily drudgery from our souls. Lovely awes us, thrills us, stands us in amazement, and puts a "Wow!" in our lives.

I am surprised sometimes by how much people miss in life by not looking outside themselves. When our sons were little, we often heard a song on *Sesame Street* that talked about how we can miss seeing a rainbow or a sunset or a shooting star because we are looking at cracks in the sidewalk and tin cans by the side of the road.

Many of us never look up or even around ourselves to be awed by all that is lovely in nature. Catch a jar of lightning bugs on a summer night and watch them light up a child's face in the darkness – that's lovely. Watch a bluebird fly in and out of a box with straw and strings and lay little turquoise eggs – that's lovely, too. Watch an inch worm measuring your finger or the dewdrops twinkling at sunrise on a spider's intricate web – both are lovely. View the play of light and shadow in a Rembrandt painting or the vivid colors splashed across the canvas of an inspired, but mentally ill, Van Gogh. Listen to Beethoven's "Ninth" or Dvorak's "New World Symphony" or even to the lilting melodies of Scotland and Ireland. The world is full of the lovely, the inspiring, the uplifting – all of it, whether in nature or from talented artists and musicians, is from God.

Whatever Is Admirable

Admirable is also translated as "good report" (KJV); "good repute" (NASB); "kind, winsome, gracious" (AMPLIFIED). Paul defines the last trait for our thoughts by adding two more words to describe it: that which is admirable is also excellent or praiseworthy. In other words, we must be cognizant of what the world admires as being worthy of praise if we are to be ambassadors for Christ.

Even without the Bible as a guide, the world knows virtuous living. The ancient Greek philosopher, Aristotle, clearly defined a set of virtues with which the citizens of Philippi in Paul's day would have been familiar. Virtue, according to Aristotle, "is a quality of character by which individuals habitually recognize and do the right thing." He divided all virtue into four categories:

• fortitude – the strength of mind and courage to persevere in the face of adversity;

• temperance – self-discipline, the control of all unruly human passions and appetites;

• justice – fairness, honesty, lawfulness and the ability to keep one's promises;

• prudence, the master virtue – practical wisdom and the ability to make the right choice in specific situations (Woodward 38-39).

None of these worldly virtues violates the Scriptures; the Bible teaches all of them.

Even today's world admires virtuous living. One of the most famous and widely used books on relationships in the business world is Dale Carnegie's *How to Win Friends and Influence People*. His secular principles easily translate into Christian principles. For example, his first chapter is titled "If You Want to Gather Honey, Don't Kick Over the Beehive." It is a worldly version of Paul's letter to the Philippians. We can't influence others to be Christians if we do not relate to them in a loving, gentle, peaceful way.

If we live according to the Scriptures in dealing with our fellowmen, we will never violate the virtuous ideals that the secular world has set in place. However, it is not for our own praise and admiration that we demonstrate these virtues, but for the glory of Christ. We are set apart and "our citizenship is in heaven" (Philippians 3:20). No matter what our vocation is, we are told to "work at it with all [our] heart, as working for the Lord, not for men" (Colossians 3:23). This Christian work ethic may win us many secular awards, honors and praise, but our ultimate award awaits us in heaven.

Paul tells the Philippian church (and us) to put into practice whatever "you have learned or received or heard from me, or seen in me." Our reward will be that "the God of peace" will be with us (4:9) guarding our hearts and minds (v. 7).

A CLEARER FOCUS

1. In this age of moral relativism, what are some things that used to be considered true by most of the religious world, but no longer are?

2. Name some American citizens whom you consider to be noble. Choose some from our early history and some from the present time. Why do you think they deserve to be called noble? Why is it harder to be perceived as having noble character in today's world?

3. How have good manners and etiquette changed in your lifetime? Why is it important for us to practice acceptable etiquette and to teach our children etiquette?

4. What are some practices that we might excuse by saying, "Everybody does it"? Are these practices okay for a Christian?

5. Give some examples of what you consider to be "lovely."

6. Should a Christian strive for worldly awards and acclaim? Why or why not?

ABOVE AND BEYOND

What do you spend most of your time thinking about? Are most of your thoughts centered on things that are true, noble, right, pure, lovely and admirable? Which of these qualities do you think about most often? Spend some time thinking about your thought patterns. If you find a glitch in your thinking, try to remove it.

SETTING OUR COURSE
BY A HIGH STAR

Philippians 4:10-20

"By a high star our course is set,
Our end is Life. Put out to Sea."
– Louis MacNiece

Paul's thank-you letter to the Philippians draws to a close. His love and appreciation for these brothers and sisters in Christ are evident as he thanks them, specifically in Chapter 4, for their gifts and their concern for him. The warm relationship between Paul and the Philippians is evident throughout the letter, but it is stated even more personally in this final chapter.

Two of Paul's most memorable statements are found here. In Philippians 4:11 he tells them that he has "learned to be content whatever the circumstances." He says, "I know what it is to be in need, and I know what it is to have plenty. I have learned the secret of being content in any and every situation" (v. 12). And then he concludes this train of thought with a sentence that has been stamped on bookmarks, framed and hung on walls, and certainly embroidered on every Christian's heart: "I can do all things through Christ which strengtheneth me" (v. 13 KJV).

Although he always sought to do God's Will with zeal, this contented Paul seems almost alien in disposition to the earlier Saul/Paul. Remember, this was the man who held the coats of the angry mob stoning Stephen (Acts 7:58; 8:1). He was also the man who was "breathing out murderous threats" (9:1) and traveling on the road to Damascus to bring more Christians before the Jewish courts to face judgment (v. 2).

As a new evangelist, he was a ferocious, inflamed Paul. He is described in his early ministry as debating with the Grecian Jews and preaching "fearlessly" and "boldly in the name of Lord" (Acts 9:27-29). He vehemently labeled Elymas "a child of the devil and an enemy of everything that is right!" (13:10), and he had no time for quitters like John Mark. In fact, his "sharp disagreement" with his fellow missionary, Barnabas, over this matter sent them separate ways (15:37-40).

Paul also publicly rebuked Peter for hypocrisy when he shunned the Gentile Christians in the presence of Jewish Christians (Galatians 2:14). Even in the Philippian letter, Paul kindles a momentary spark of his earlier fire when he calls the Jewish Christians who were demanding circumcision "dogs" (3:2). Paul was never one to condone error through silence, yet the Paul of the Philippian letter is a more contented, warmer individual than is seen in his letters to other congregations. At the time of penning the Philippian letter, he is in his late 50s. In fact, in his letter to Philemon written the year before, he refers to himself as "an old man" (v. 9). The fire has not gone out, but the searing heat at this point in his life has settled down to the warm glow of a hearth fire.

How does Paul find this secret of contentment? How does he come to trust so fully in the strength of Christ despite his imprisonment and possible execution? The answers to these questions can be found by re-examining the principles taught in the Philippian letter, principles upon which Paul's daily life is based, transforming him into that contented person he has now become. He tells the Christians at Philippi (and us) not only to imitate Christ (2:5) but also to imitate him (3:17; 4:9). The life of Paul is a pathway to peace and contentment for all of us.

Pathway to Contentment
• *Wisdom From Experience.* Part of the answer simply can be found in the wisdom that comes in older years. For this reason, bishops or shep-

herds are also called elders, and the qualifications given for them demand life experiences associated with maturity (1 Timothy 3:1-7; Titus 1:6-9). Much can be said for the contentment that comes in later life after years of prayerful communication with God and deep, meditative study of His Word. Material possessions are certainly less important.

A speaker in our summer series came to our home for a meal before the evening worship. He was an older gentleman, a retired minister and college Bible professor who had never before visited us. As usual, I dusted, polished and cleaned the house, making sure that everything was spotless. After all, everyone who comes to our house generally compliments either its unusual structure (the hand-hewn beams) or the colorful decor. However, this man was not impressed; in fact, he didn't even notice his surroundings. Although this happened years ago, I still remember being awed by his heart and mind, so focused on spirituality that physical trappings meant little to him. He taught me an unspoken lesson about the contentment to be found in holiness.

We cannot ignore God in our youth without some regret marring our contentment in later years. The preacher in Ecclesiastes tells us, "Remember your Creator in the days of your youth" (12:1). He concludes the book with "the whole duty of man": "Fear God and keep his commandments" (v. 13). Some of us will not live long enough to gain the wisdom of old age; therefore, if we are to assimilate any of the contentment of which Paul speaks in our lives, we must begin now, not later.

Young women with children often say, "I'm just too busy – I don't have time" for a daily quiet period of meditation and prayer. Admittedly, during child-rearing years it is difficult, but if we truly have a desire to nurture our souls, we will make time, whether it be in the early hours before everyone else in our household is up, in the late hours after everyone else is in bed, or during the children's nap time. Hopefully, our husbands, who also need a meditative period, will take over home duties to give us the same quiet time. No matter the method, personal meditation and prayer are essential to spiritual growth. Without it, we are an empty shell going through meaningless motion, and we may never again have an opportunity to fill our cup with contentment.

• ***Close Christian Friends.*** Paul was contented, also, because he surrounded himself with men and women of like faith. In his early ministry, he worked with Barnabas and later with Silas. He came to know and love his "true son in the faith," Timothy (1 Timothy 1:1) and mentions by name many other Christians who were close to him (i.e., Epaphroditus, Euodia, Syntyche and Clement in Philippians). Assuredly, those whom Paul specifically names are on his heart as our brothers and sisters in Christ should be on ours. However, we cannot be "united with Christ" and in "fellowship with the Spirit" nor can we be "like-minded, having the same love, being one in spirit and purpose" (Philippians 2:1-2) with people we don't know. Furthermore, we cannot know people with whom we have not spent time.

Although we must all have friends in the world (to whom we are an example), our closest and dearest friends should be among our Christian family. Like Paul, we must know their names and be a part of their lives, sharing joy and sorrow, heartache and triumph, hope and concern, all in common love. We cannot withdraw ourselves from the fellowship of the saints and "give up meeting together" (Hebrews 10:25) and at the same time "work out [our] salvation with fear and trembling" (Philippians 2:12). We cannot crucify "the Son of God all over again" (Hebrews 6:6) and expect His strength to comfort us when we face the sufferings of life or the infirmities of old age. True contentment comes not only in our own personal communing with God but also in the sharing of that communion with others of like faith.

• *Humble Recognition of God's Grace.* Paul's contentment also comes from his humility. He never takes his salvation for granted. Knowing that he once was a person who persecuted Christ and His church through his misguided legalistic righteousness, he does not take the gift of salvation lightly. He tells the Philippians, "I want to know Christ and the power of his resurrection and the fellowship of sharing in his sufferings, becoming like him in his death, and so, somehow, to attain the resurrection from the dead" (Philippians 3:10). Therefore, he presses "on toward the goal to win the prize" (v. 14) because he has not yet reached it. Paul understands that the Christian race is a lifetime commitment; he never retires from serving others but encourages them to follow in his footsteps as he follows Christ. He is willing to be "poured out like a drink offering" (2:17) and is torn between his desire to go on to his heavenly reward and his need to stay on earth and continue to produce fruit for the Lord: "For to me, to live is Christ and to die is gain" (1:21-23).

Louie, a retired elder in our congregation, was torn between his desire for his heavenly reward and his fruit-bearing here on earth. Illness had forced his retirement from the eldership but not from the Lord's work. He missed church much of the time, but when he was able, he dragged his oxygen cart behind him and took his place on the pew. Everyone knew when Louie thought the preacher had made a particularly eloquent point by his firm "Amen." Although he was no longer able to teach a Sunday school class, he was the most prepared student there. Louie also took special interest in the young people at church and, when confined at home, built an ark of the covenant and a tabernacle to scale in his woodshop for teaching the children.

Louie regretted having wasted the early years of his life. Just two weeks before he died, he asked me to e-mail this message to a foreign exchange student who had lived with us and had accepted Christ in baptism while in the United States:

> Tell her she needs to keep her eye on Jesus. She will understand as she gets older just how much more rhythm her spiritual body will attain. I ask the Lord every day to forgive me for not really realizing that sooner in life. You had better believe I now know just what it means to solely depend on God for my day to day existence.

When Louie died, he requested no flowers; on his casket was his pall – his well-worn, note-filled Bible opened to his favorite scripture. Through weakness and through death, Louie taught us all that Christ will give us the strength to accept whatever may come if we give our lives completely over to Him.

The Christian's life begins with our baptismal birth. It has no end because our reward is eternal life. Like Paul, we must be totally dependent on God, knowing that we, too, have undeservedly received the gift of salvation through God's grace. We must be truthful in our self-evaluation, checking our hearts and minds for wrongful motives and replacing whatever is evil or false with thoughts that are true, noble, right, pure, lovely and admirable. We must humbly accept the suffering that comes our way, knowing that we will be shaped and molded by it into more complete servants of Christ, empowered by the empathy we need to help others. Ultimately, like Paul and the Philippians, we will "shine like stars in the universe as [we] hold out the word of life" (Philippians 2:15-16). Then, when our work is complete, we can say, "Oh, God, make small / The old star-eaten blanket of the sky, / That I may fold it round me and in comfort lie" (Thomas Ernest Hulme).

A CLEARER FOCUS

1. What differences have you observed in spirituality and disposition in younger Christians when comparing them to older Christians? Why do these differences exist?

2. Examine the qualifications of elders in 1 Timothy 3:1-7 and Titus 1:6-9 and their wives in 1 Timothy 3:11. Which of these traits should we all display as mature Christians?

3. Give other practical suggestions for young mothers needing time for personal spiritual growth.

4. Do you know the names of everyone in your congregation? What can we do to improve our congregational efforts to become more personal and involved in each other's lives?

5. Have you become more spiritual through this study of the Philippian letter? What overt actions have you taken that demonstrate this spiritual growth?

ABOVE AND BEYOND

Dear reader, please take Paul's letter to the Philippians to heart. I have learned so much by writing this study book, and I have seen some changes in my life as a result. You will, too, if you let the Word work in your life.

Many people call Philippians the book of joy, but joy is not possible without attention to another theme that threads its way through his entire message. Paul wants each one of us, like the Philippians, to make our relationship with God a very personal one. No more pretense. No more just going to church. No shallow "a little dab will do you" religion. Our whole hearts and minds must be saturated with the spirituality that comes only through focusing our entire being on Christ and His Word. Our joy and peace and contentment cannot be plastered on like a facade; they must be in the building itself. Only then will they pour forth from the windows of our souls as a light to beckon others to Christ and make them want what we have.

WORKS CITED

American Heritage Dictionary of the English Language. New College Ed. Boston: Houghton Mifflin, 1976.

Barker, Kenneth, ed. *The NIV Study Bible.* Grand Rapids: Zondervan, 1985.

Bartlett's Quotations. Bartleby.com: Great Books Online. 20 Aug. 2003 <http://www.bartleby.com>.

Caffin, B.C., Ed. "Philippians." *The Pulpit Commentary.* Vol. 20. Eds. H.D.M. Spence and Joseph S. Exell. Grand Rapids: Eerdmans, 1980.

Carnegie, Dale. *How to Win Friends and Influence People.* New York: Pocket Books, 1981.

Chambers, Dan. *Showtime! Worship in the Age of Show Business.* Nashville: 21st Century Christian, 1997.

Clarke, Adam. *Adam Clarke's Commentary on the Bible.* Abr. by Ralph Earle. Grand Rapids: Baker, 1974.

Comparative Study Bible. Grand Rapids: Zondervan, 1999.

Elwell, Walter A. *Baker Topical Guide to the Bible (NIV).* Grand Rapids: Baker Books, 1991.

Klaus, Peggy. *Brag! – The Art of Tooting Your Own Horn Without Blowing It.* Warner Books, 2003. <www.klausact.com/services/training.html>.

Lipscomb, David. *A Commentary on the New Testament Epistles: Ephesians, Philippians, and Colossians.* Vol. 9. Ed. J.W. Shepherd. Nashville: Gospel Advocate, 1989.

Nelson's Three-in-One Bible Reference Companion. Nashville: Thomas Nelson, 1982.

Osbeck, Kenneth W. *101 Hymn Stories.* Grand Rapids: Kregel, 1982.

"Pictorial Library of Bible Lands: Greece and Rome." BiblePlaces.com. 28 May 2003. <http://www.bibleplaces.com>.

Price, Brian R. "A Code of Chivalry: Modern, Based on the 'Old Code.'" April 1997. *The Knighthood, Chivalry, and Tournaments Resource Library.* Discovery Channel School. 4 Aug. 2003. <http://www.chronique.com>.

Shakespeare, William. *Macbeth. Elements of Literature: Sixth Course.* Robert Anderson et al. Austin: Harcourt, 1993.

Swindoll, Charles R. *The Tale of the Tardy Oxcart: And 1,301 Other Stories.* Nashville: Word, 1984.

Wiegand, John P., ed. *Praise for the Lord.* Nashville: Mark M. McInteer, 1997.

"What You Should Know About Obesity in Children and Adolescents." *The Brown University Child and Adolescent Behavior Letter* 19.5 (2003).

Woodward, Kenneth L. "What Is Virtue?" *Newsweek.* 13 June 1994: 38-39.